The Instant of Knowing

POETS ON POETRY

David Lehman, General Editor
Donald Hall, Founding Editor

New titles

Tess Gallagher, *Soul Barnacles*
Linda Gregerson, *Negative Capability*
Larry Levis, *The Gazer Within*
William Matthews, *The Poetry Blues*
Charles Simic, *A Fly in the Soup*

Recently published

Rachel Hadas, *Merrill, Cavafy, Poems, and Dreams*
Yusef Komunyakaa, *Blue Notes*
Philip Larkin, *Required Writing*
Alicia Suskin Ostriker, *Dancing at the Devil's Party*
Ron Padgett, *The Straight Line*

Also available are collections by

A. R. Ammons, Robert Bly, Philip Booth, Marianne Boruch, Hayden Carruth, Fred Chappell, Amy Clampitt, Tom Clark, Douglas Crase, Robert Creeley, Donald Davie, Peter Davison, Tess Gallagher, Suzanne Gardinier, Allen Grossman, Thom Gunn, John Haines, Donald Hall, Joy Harjo, Robert Hayden, Edward Hirsch, Daniel Hoffman, Jonathan Holden, John Hollander, Andrew Hudgins, Josephine Jacobsen, Weldon Kees, Galway Kinnell, Mary Kinzie, Kenneth Koch, John Koethe, Richard Kostelanetz, Maxine Kumin, Martin Lammon (editor), David Lehman, Philip Levine, John Logan, William Logan, William Matthews, William Meredith, Jane Miller, Carol Muske, Geoffrey O'Brien, Gregory Orr, Marge Piercy, Anne Sexton, Charles Simic, Louis Simpson, William Stafford, Anne Stevenson, May Swenson, James Tate, Richard Tillinghast, Diane Wakoski, C. K. Williams, Alan Williamson, Charles Wright, and James Wright

Josephine Jacobsen

The Instant of Knowing

LECTURES, CRITICISM, AND OCCASIONAL PROSE

Edited by Elizabeth Spires

Ann Arbor

THE UNIVERSITY OF MICHIGAN PRESS

First paperback edition 2002

Published in the United States of America by
The University of Michigan Press
Manufactured in the United States of America
♾ Printed on acid-free paper

2005 2004 2003 2002 5 4 3 2

A CIP catalog record for this book is available from the British Library.

Library of Congress Cataloging-in-Publication Data

Jacobsen, Josephine.
[Selections. 1998]
The instant of knowing : lectures, criticism, and occasional prose / edited by Elizabeth Spires.
p. cm. — (Poets on poetry)
Includes bibliographical references (p.).
ISBN 0-472-09660-5 (cloth).—ISBN 0-472-06660-9 (paper)
1. Jacobsen, Josephine—Authorship. 2. Poetry—Authorship. 3. Poetics. I. Spires, Elizabeth. II. Title. III. Series.
PS 3519.A424Z469 1998
811'.52—dc21 97-27974
CIP

ISBN 0-472-06660-9 (pbk. : alk. paper)

ACKNOWLEDGMENTS

The author and editor wish to thank the following people for their help in compiling this book: Charlotte Blaylock, Evelyn Prettyman, Ann LoLordo, Mary Rogers, and Nancy Norris; and for valuable technical assistance, Madison Smartt Bell.

Grateful acknowledgment is made to the following journals and publishers for permission to reprint previously published materials: American Voice, Associated University Presses, Atlanta Review, Baltimore Sun, Commonweal, Gettysburg Review, The Library of Congress, and *Longstreet Press.* The poems "Voyage" and "Program" first appeared in the *New Yorker* and are reprinted by permission. "In the Beginning" by Daniel Hoffman is from his book *A Little Geste* (New York: Oxford University Press, 1960). Copyright © 1960 by Daniel Hoffman and reprinted by permission of the author. Every effort has been made to trace the ownership of all copyrighted material in this book and to obtain permission for its use.

for Joseph Gallagher

—J. J.

Contents

Introduction *Elizabeth Spires* 1

I. Memoir and Lectures

Statement on Poetry 9
Lion under Maples 10
From Anne to Marianne: Some Women in American Poetry 22
The Instant of Knowing 39
One Poet's Poetry 50
The Admiring Bog 61

II. Reviews and Criticism

Frost, Cummings, Williams: Legacy of Three Poets 75
Poet of the Particular 84
History as Death 93
Corsons Inlet 96
Stories and "Texts" by Samuel Beckett 99
The Felicity of J. D. Salinger 101

III. Travel and Op-Ed Pieces

Atlantic City Glowed like a Jewel 109
Never Was the Play the Thing 113
Happily in Transit, Transported 116

A Kind of Beginning 119
The Meaning of Arrival 122
Where the Wild Went About 125
The Swamp's Talk 128
More White than Feathers 131
The Traveler 134
The Handless Clock 137
Why You Not Say Good Morning? 140
Openness, a Vast Confusion 143
Breaking Bread Together 146
International Aspects of the Mad Hatter 149
Mayed and Traught on a Desert Island 152
To Our Waiting Names 155
Artifacts of Memory 158
Time Out of Mind 161
A Generous Disorder 164
Trees 167
A Day of One's Own 170

IV. An Interview and Four Poems

The Sisters 175
A Conversation with Her Sister 177
Voyage 206
Program 207
Piazza di Spagna 208

Introduction

Elizabeth Spires

Art is long, and life is short. Or is it the other way around? On the evidence of over sixty-five years of literary productivity, both art and life have been long and rewarding for Josephine Jacobsen.

The life's work of a greatly gifted poet may not offer the suspense of a well-plotted novel, but there is still a certain drama in seeing the arc of thought and accomplishment fitted between the covers of one book. Reading Josephine Jacobsen's most recent poetry collection, *In the Crevice of Time: New and Collected Poems* (1995) is akin to watching some frightening or wondrous natural process, say a tree or flower blooming, captured in time-lapse photography—from the first stirrings of a germinal impulse to the rapid movement into individuality, maturity, and inevitable denouement. It's a disturbingly compressed tale of birth, change, growth, and oblivion. So it is with Josephine Jacobsen, who, at eighty-eight, continues to write with extraordinary force and passion. Like the aging, prescient figure in "Hourglass," a recent poem, "She perfectly understands the calendar / and the sun's passage. But she grips the leash / and leans on the air that is hers and here."

Unlike many of her poetic contemporaries, Jacobsen did not pursue a particularly literary life. Born in 1908, she was part of a generation that included Lowell, Bishop, Berryman, and Roethke. Her formal education ended with her graduation from high school. In an interview with John Wheatcroft, included here, she talks about her mother's decision against sending her to college (Jacobsen's father had died when she was five). Calling the theater—along with poetry—"her great love," she acted with the Vagabond Players in Baltimore until she married in her twenties and had a son, Erlend. The marriage, to Eric Jacobsen, was a rich and sustaining one, lasting sixty-two years, until his death in 1995.

Jacobsen's first four collections of poetry, *Let Each Man Remember* (1940), *For the Unlost* (1946), *The Human Climate* (1953), and *The Animal Inside* (1966), published by smaller presses outside the circle of New York, did not establish her as a major poet of her generation, although by all rights they should have. She did not teach, nor was she deeply involved with the literary world, until she was named Consultant in Poetry to the Library of Congress in 1971, when she was sixty-three. For the most part, her writing was done on the side, in brief intense spurts during isolated months at Yaddo and MacDowell, and during winter stays in the Caribbean, a locale to which she has always felt attracted (and that provides the setting for some of the travel pieces included here) because of its "wonderful sense of strangeness . . . which was totally other."

With the publication of *The Shade Seller* in 1974 and *The Chinese Insomniacs* in 1981, Jacobsen became better known; in the past ten years she has received a flurry of accolades, including such honors as the Lenore Marshall Award for *The Sisters* in 1988, the annual fellowship of the Academy of American Poets, the Shelley Memorial Award from the Poetry Society of America in 1993, and election to the American Academy of Arts and Letters in 1994 (the only poet and only woman elected that year). *In the Crevice of Time: New and Collected Poems,* a nominee for the National Book Award in Poetry in 1995, subsequently received the Poets' Prize, and, in 1997, Jacobsen's lifetime achievement in poetry was recognized by the Poetry Society of America with the Robert Frost Medal, its highest honor. With the publication of *What Goes Without Saying: Collected Stories* (1996), and, now, *The Instant of Knowing: Lectures, Criticism, and Occasional Prose,* the best of Jacobsen's poetry, fiction, and nonfiction is finally available in three volumes.

Throughout her career Jacobsen has persistently chosen to write poems of an unnervingly pure lyric intensity. She is a formal poet with the ability, when she wants to and the poem demands it, to write in finely controlled free verse. She has, unfashionably, always been clear in her refusal to use personal, intimate experience in a direct or explicit way in her poems. What one observes in Jacobsen's poetry is experience worked into the fabric of the poem, in its tone and stance, rather than experience overtly disclosed. A Josephine Jacobsen poem will not come alive for the reader until this texture is both intellectually processed and viscerally felt, the way meaning in spoken conversation is understood as much through a shift in inflection as by simple denotation. Readers who prefer topical poems will go away from Jacobsen dissatisfied, because her concerns are not so easily categorized. In her poems and prose she is part traveler ("Born travelers must and will have terra incognita"), part archaeologist ("We breathe through our future. / *Remember me* is the message"), and part seer ("I know all about what is / happening in this city at just / this moment; every last grain of dark I conceive").

Initially, Jacobsen moved through a period of literary influence, trying out various modes and styles, both romantic and modern, her chief influences being Yeats and Auden. But by the age of forty, when many poets privately wonder, "What now?" Jacobsen had stepped out from the shadow of influence and the confinement of closed forms to begin writing the poems that are most her own. In such masterful poems as "Instances of Communication" and "Poems for My Cousin" Jacobsen presents the physical world as a place of potential symbol and metaphor, a place where divine speech—the speech of poetry and prayer—can exist. Working outside of any poetic circle, she said of the process, "I was forced . . . to develop a sense of my own intention." And her intention, from almost the beginning, was to write poetry in which "the experience, wherever found, is the experience of being taken out of oneself, simultaneous with an inner penetration to unity. In that respect, the aesthetic experience is similar to the religious experience, and vice versa."

A few years later, she began to write reviews, lectures, and essays, contributing pieces to the *Commonweal,* the *Nation,* the *Washington Post,* the *Baltimore Sun,* and other publications. The best of these constitute the present volume. Circling back to her early interest in the theater, she also collaborated with William Mueller on two well-received critical books about contemporary playwrights: *The Testament of Samuel Beckett* (1964) and *Ionesco and Genet: Playwrights of Silence* (1968).

As literary commentator, Jacobsen writes with refreshing candor. Born long before feminism was the rage, and leading an apparently conventional life as wife and mother, she was, from the beginning, sympathetic to the difficulties facing earlier generations of women writers and artists in America. In her lecture "From Anne to Marianne: Some Women in American Poetry" she asks, "What were the chief elements in the attitudes of American women poets in the long desert stretching between Anne Bradstreet and Emily Dickinson?" Her answer is unequivocal and provocative: "The chief elements . . . were those one might expect from a body of literate, highly privileged slaves. In general, life is seen as something to be endured; emotion as something foredoomed; death as a release, even for the young. . . . The constants in the lives of women poets in the first hundred and fifty years on this continent were endurance, faith (often less as a conviction than as a desperate refuge), and a courage that was less ardent than fatalistic." In contrast, in "A Day of One's Own" she extols the virtues of artists' colonies as havens where the imagination—"the active, secret subterranean life," as she calls it—of the contemporary woman artist can have free rein.

For Jacobsen, the making of art, the writing of a poem, is a form of consolation in a time-bound world. In the title poem of the collection *In the Crevice of Time,* she describes the moment when a "hunter-priest" made the first cave painting, "his art an act of faith, his grave / an act of art: for all, / for all, a celebration and a burial." The poem connects the human urge to make art to the fact of our death. It is a theme that recurs in such pieces as "Artifacts of Memory," a prose meditation that takes in Pompeii and the cave paintings of Lascaux. Art, for the poet, connects us to the timeless and eternal, even as it depicts the twinned, inseparable aspects of temporal existence: its joy *and* terror. The idea of "terror, surmounted by joy" (the phrase occurs in her poem "The Enemy of the Herds, the Lion") infuses much of Jacobsen's writing and is central to understanding what she is about as a poet.

A celebratory tone pervades much of the present volume, as Jacobsen affirms our deep, unspoken need for art and literature. In the essay "Lion under Maples" she writes: "If one tries for one moment to truly imagine a world in which poetry, in the deepest sense, is nonexistent—why, that is Hell, nor are we out of it. It would so rob the senses and drain the mind that one of those ashy lunar landscapes would show in comparison as fruitful." The sentiment is reiterated and expanded in "Never Was the Play the Thing," in which her preference for all that is human wins out over the "virtual" world of technology that we seem to be heading toward: "Computers . . . will reveal possibilities I can barely imagine. But nothing, absolutely nothing, can threaten that electric contact, that almost physical union, in which flesh-and-blood human beings, now, at this very moment, tell us and show us, and ask us to believe. And fondly, naively, I believe we are indispensable—that no canned laughter can substitute for that risky, moment-to-moment collaboration. The magician's trick may fail; the actor may blank out; someone in the audience may faint. Maybe no one will laugh—maybe there won't be that special stretched hush at the climactic scene. It is not settled. It is alive. It has not been packaged."

Now eighty-eight, Jacobsen continues to live and write in Baltimore. This volume ends with an interview and three recent poems, completed since the publication of *In the Crevice of Time.* At the time Jacobsen was writing "Piazza di Spagna," the poem that concludes this book, she darkly insisted in a letter to me that it would be her last. I'm happy to report that the prediction was premature and that she is currently at work on new poems. Her readers await them.

I
Memoir and Lectures

Statement on Poetry

I don't really value very highly "statements" from a poet in regard to her work. I can perhaps best introduce my own poetry by saying what I have not done, rather than defining what I have done. I have not involved my work with any clique, school, or other group: I have tried not to force any poem into an overall concept of "how I write poetry" when it should be left to create organically its own individual style; I have not been content to repeat what I have already accomplished or to establish any stance that would limit the flexibility of discovery. I have not confused technical innovation, however desirable, with poetic originality or intensity. I have not utilized poetry as a social or political lever. I have not conceded that any subject matter, any vocabulary, any approach, or any form is in itself necessarily unsuitable to the uses of poetry. I have not tried to establish a reputation as a poet on any grounds but those of my poetry.

Quoted by Joseph Parisi in *Contemporary Poets,* ed. James Vinson and D. L. Kirkpatrick, 4th ed. (New York: St. Martin's Press, 1985), 425.

Lion under Maples

Beginnings are hard to trace. When did the root first push up, when did the first leaf show red? And the beginnings of poetry—anyone's poetry—are even more ambiguous. In a thought? An impression, an emotion? A word? Sometimes—rarely, but sometimes—a total scene rises out of the long confusion of memory. A scene saturated with something previously unexperienced, something so penetrating that its flavor can be faintly tasted decades and decades later.

If I had to specify the first touch or first consciousness of the impulse that later became the practice of poetry, I would find three scenes, altogether unrelated to the literary in which so many poets have been touched by a premonitory finger. The experience, wherever found, is the experience of being taken out of oneself, simultaneous with an inner penetration to unity. In that respect the aesthetic experience is similar to the religious experience, and vice versa. For me, as a child, two of these experiences were arboreal; the other occurred deep in the grasses of a small meadow. None was connected with another human, and, with the fine contempt for logic that poetry often evinces, the poetry of which these were perhaps the initial conscious, though unidentified, seed had little to do overtly with nature poetry and everything to do with the human being.

The first was in the branches of a dogwood, one of three white dogwoods on the slope of a lawn. A child of five or six, in the crotch of two branches, muffled by thick leaves and the

---

From *The Confidence Woman: Twenty-Six Women Writers at Work,* ed. Eve Shelnutt (Atlanta, GA: Longstreet Press, 1991).

flawed, slightly curved blossoms, their white tinged with a faint green. In the fall the tree would be frantic with birds after the red berries, but at the moment the green is a motionless cloud. And I am motionless too, secretly out of the lawn, the sun, the tree itself; still, absolutely attentive, without expectation. There is just this moment, with the lawn and tree inside it, and all of them inside me. The only thing that is happening is interior, and that is happening in an interior motionlessness.

Then it is another tree, a North Carolina tree, a tall, fluid long-leaf pine. The branches are slimmer, so that I have to hold more tightly, and there are bright beads of resin on the smooth bark. The long fringy blue-green needles hang thickly, and when the air, which smells of the resin on my fingers, moves through them, there is a great sustained sigh. The bough itself even moves very slightly. And again something important and untranslatable has this as its center. The third is in a very small meadow, probably in July, a meadow on a hill above the lawn of a New England cottage. I am down in plumy grasses over my head, and the yellow and white and red of wildflowers (not yet known as buttercups and daisies and devil's paintbrush) are scattered above me. There is a faint humming. Gnats? Or bees? Or other insects?

Again the problem is that I am experiencing acutely something for which I have no words but which requires response. There is compulsion to respond, but no speech I have ever heard is possible. This creates a tension, a pressure simultaneously from without and within, and the moment, neither short nor long, is endless. Later, this will identify itself as the language, if it can be found, of the poem. It will never be quite accurate, but it will be unmistakable. So that I will later learn that every impulse that creates this sensation comes from the strangeness of some familiar thing, a face, a motion, a sound, which must be translated into a vocabulary produced from within. That was the wordless impulse that required expression. I have wondered if the totally different locales were connected with not only my peripatetic childhood but also with the ranging locales and situations of my poetry. A rooted provenance has been vital to the work of so many writers. Vital to mine, though many roots came later, was the sense of the unexpected, the unfamiliar, the swift or slow shock of major differences, to be understood and interpreted.

I know that my first encounter with the magic of words as a formula of their power came early. I had a black nurse, one of the two people I most loved. We spent a great deal of time—most of my time, actually—together. Alice was companion, friend, judge, recourse, and pleasure.

In the evening I was put to bed just, it seemed to me, as everything mysterious and worthwhile was about to happen. It was then, I was sure, that exhilarating and mysterious things began, in a life to which I would someday have access. On the other hand, my familiar bed was comforting in a way, secure and warm. This was in a beachfront hotel, and I would have said goodnight to my mother, who came up after dinner for that ceremony, radiant and more beautiful than I then realized. That vision, like daylight, would be gone. I would say formally, "Now I lay me down to sleep" . . . Alice would put out the light and stand in the bright hall doorway and say, "Sweet dreams. . . ." It didn't have a positive meaning; she never thought of my dreams as sweet or otherwise. They were just things that happened to people when they went to sleep. But "sweet dreams" was something different. It was a powerful rite, implicit with both formality and magic. It was the seal of the day, the threshold to sleep, the equivalent of the town crier's "All's well!"

On rare occasions my conduct in some undreamed-of particular would have been so bad—not what was reasonably expected of me—that some form of retribution was essential in the nature of things. Then Alice would not say, "Sweet dreams." Everything unraveled. The dark became hostile, the door a drawbridge about to rise. First annoyed, then tense, then fearful, I would plead. "Good night," said Alice. But no, no, no, no "Sweet dreams!" I pleaded, and, being kind, as well as judicial, after a feverish short or long struggle, the vital syllables discharged me into sleep.

In the dogwood, the long-leaf pine, the August meadow, I learned what I did not understand: that there were experiences for which my everyday speech did not serve. It would be years before William Carlos Williams's words told me, "You have no other language for it than the poem." But I already knew.

It would be years before I understood that certain words in combination could seize and control the emotions as though hypnotic. But I knew then.

Younger than this, I learned about ambiguity, that frightening and precious light by which the writer sees, according to the lighting, quite different interpretations of a human face, a human action.

I was in the house with the dogwoods on the lawn; young enough to be in a stroller. Around my shoulders I had some sort of curly cape (astrakhan?), which tickled my chin. Alice was pushing me down a little lane, off the small main road, with high prickly bushes—I suppose they were wild blackberries or raspberries—on either side and small leafy trees shading us. If the cape was an astrakhan, it could not have been summer, and, if the trees were leafy, not winter. Autumn? Around a little curve, directly before us, a figure loomed—a scruffy man, with red pinpoint eyes, a stain-colored nose, and dirty trousers. He was right on top of us. Had he been lying down, or had he turned to walk out?

Alice gave a sort of modified howl, whirled the stroller around, and pelted back down the lane, while I bounced and clutched. No one followed us. But even in the road we kept up our flight. I had never gone so fast.

I had neither the time nor the wit to be frightened, but Alice was very frightened indeed. I don't know whether she thought we were going to be murdered or I was going to be kidnapped or if she was only shocked and scared to find social impropriety so close to the lawn and the rhododendrons and dogwoods. At home was much excitement, and though I still hadn't the material from which to produce this kind of fright, I was imbued with the sense of a sinister adventure. The picture of the ugly, disheveled man so close to us, and evidently so threatening, made an immense impression, and today I can summon up the figure, which now irresistibly reminds me of a Beckett figure or a circus clown.

Was he sinister? Or pathetic? Or drunk? Or lost?

I have thought often of how much more instructive this was than one of those certified sinister encounters famous in fiction. Gradually, it surrounded itself with options, with possibilities; it was pregnant with ambiguity.

My initiation into another of the great literary processes came, also in a matter of minutes, when I was ten. I am not at all sure when I first tried to write a poem, but at ten I had that loss of innocence that can never be repeated. I saw a poem of mine published. Printed. In a magazine. For sale. Being bought by readers.

This event took place on Lexington Avenue and 86th Street, at a kiosk. *St. Nicholas* was then the solitary magazine for children that did not bleat at them or condescend, and I worshiped it. I had sent off a poem, a more credulous gesture than the letters thrust up the chimney en route north. I had next to no hope but a clawing excitement. Then I got a letter from the magazine, congratulating me and naming the unbelievable issue. I knew the day, if not the minute, when *St. Nicholas* arrived at the kiosk, but I had not been allowed on a New York street alone, and I needed to go by myself. After endless arguments, pleadings, pleadings, I could go—though, releasing me, the doorman was dubious.

There it was. I paid for the experience that comes only once and held the shiny cover in my hands. It was there. So immense was the shock, so penetrating to my innocence, that I can no longer remember the title *or* the subject matter, though I can recall the dismal nature of both in the case of two subsequent poems published before I reached the disqualifying age of twelve.

I stood on the sidewalk, obstructive, stunned, looking at my words, naked, displayed to the world, and happily I did not know that this deflowering would be a climax never reached again. For I was purely satisfied.

A great poet told me years later that the ego's goal is never, never reached, that the cheating mark is simply shifted ahead, and the gnawing dissatisfaction remains. But I believed, on the sidewalk of Lexington and 86th, that I had reached it, beyond all failure, and not even when a silver and then a gold badge fell upon me without recreating that initial ecstasy did I understand his truth.

The insidious quality of that moment has remained in my mind. The poem itself appeared to me differently: enhanced, anointed. The tiny creative act, dubious as it was, was buried in the satisfaction of an even more dubious proof. I did not know Emily Dickinson's frog, the Somebody who told his name all day to an admiring bog, but the kiosk rises before me regularly as I watch the slide down the slippery slope from poetry to publication, to prestige, to publicity, to . . .

I doubt if a poet who believed in him- or herself has ever lived who had no interest whatsoever in publication—that means by which a word goes out to the ears of fellow humans one will never see. But that passage can be as destructive as the poet is gullible. But how could I have believed that never again would I be so hopelessly, innocently, orgiasticly satisfied?

A favorite question of interviewers is: which poets most influenced your poetic development? It's a confusing question that is apt to trigger an inaccurate answer. Early influences—perhaps all influences—are more reflective of the state and need of the influenced than guideposts to poetic maturity. And the question of value is especially tricky, since stimulation is the seed, and stimulation comes from uncredited sources. Graham Greene remarks somewhere on the ability of a music-hall tune, under certain circumstances, to touch the emotions more sharply than a musical masterpiece.

If I have cause for gratitude, let it be to Robert Service, Rudyard Kipling; to Dante Gabriel Rossetti; to Keats, Yeats, and Donne. The last three meant nothing to me in my trance at the 86th Street kiosk. But I could passionately recite, "They're making my money diminish / I'm sick of the taste of champagne / Thank God when I'm skinned to a finish / I'll pipe for the Yukon again . . . " or, "Back of the bar in a poker game / Sat Dangerous Dan McGrew / And watching his luck was his light o'love / the lady that's known as Lou."

I graduated to "The young recruits are shaking / and they'll want their beer today / After hanging Danny Deever in the morning." There I lit up in my very bones to discover that the same pound of rhythm that had enthralled me in Service could present deadly and complicated events and dimly to perceive the distance between drama and melodrama.

But I had an unidentified craving for the lyrical and fell headlong into Rossetti, reciting to myself, "Her eyes were deeper than the depths / of waters stilled at even / She held three lilies in her hand / and the stars in her hair were seven." I quote from memory, after how many decades—probably inaccurately but not *that* inaccurately.

Then, when I was sixteen, a trumpet blast: "What lady's that / Who cloth enrich the hand of yonder knight . . . "

We were spending a month in Maine. I knew no one in Portland, except the daughter of a friend of a friend of my mother's. She was sixteen, bronzed and athletic, an expert sailor. She was civilization itself, and we behaved in a friendly fashion with each other on our three or four engagements. This left me free to read.

In the library of our rented cottage was a complete set of Shakespeare, in large print. Each play was bound in a separate volume, with clear beautiful pages. How shameful that this should be the decisive factor. We, too, had sets of Shakespeare, one enormous volume bound in calfskin, with splendid pictures and print impenetrably fine, and another in separate tiny volumes, green, with slightly foxed pages and print almost as small as the mammoth book's. The Portland set was one play to a handsome red binding, with print so clear and bold that the lines marched out. I read, before we had to leave, every single one, except *Coriolanus* and one (I forget which) of the Kings, being drawn back, in midcareer, to *Romeo and Juliet, Othello,* and *Macbeth.* At that point I had no patience with Lear, whom I regarded as a graceless and self-centered curmudgeon who didn't know a good thing when he saw it. It was years before I returned to find another man.

After this apocalyptic opening of my eyes and ears, the whole welter of English poetry broke over me. When I tried to write, as I couldn't help doing, I felt confined and frustrated. I could see very little connection between what I wrote and what I cared to read. It wasn't that I despised my own work; indeed, I was excited by, and sometimes proud of, what I had done. It was simply that it seemed so remote from certain inexpressible experiences. In one of Richard Eberhart's poems there is a phrase I have never forgotten: "the instant of knowing." That was the instant in the dogwood tree, in the pine, on the meadow grasses. That was what I needed to put into poetry and could not. I did not understand that I would never truly translate that inner wordless language; that no one did. Only later did I begin to realize that a sharp and fortunate approximation of that wordless message was what I might hope for: never willingly to distort it or manipulate it for any purpose. That my objective was to get closer to it—closer and closer. Much later, because of the stories I began to publish, and because of the characters, actions, and emotions in my poetry, I began to get requests from publishers to see a novel. Knowing what you cannot do is a writer's second best gift, the best being a hard quick glimpse of what you must try for. Long before I was familiar with Poe's dicta, or had had comment on my own short stories, I knew that the satisfaction of compression, of the immediate that ties to the timeless, was what I had to have. If there were to be a design over and under the design, it had to be so vital that, ripped out, the fabric would unravel. So I concentrated on mining my vertical vein, my immediate, related moment.

I used docilely to try to examine my relations with the poetry I had read, that of the past, of the present. And, finally, I realized that the relationship of the reader to the best poetry is like that of a promiscuous but perceptive lover who, though he falls perpetually in and out of love, retains the friendship of ex-lovers and cannot predict what tone, what accent, what movement, at any given time, will compel him. He will indeed outgrow certain loves, but his unpredictability, his capacity to be entranced by a new discovery, to weary of a still-admired favorite, to rediscover the impact of something long abandoned, will be endless. The degree of intimacy between the reader and the poem, then, probably has less to do with the poem's offering than with the reader's experienced need. There are moments in which an anonymous quatrain—say "Western wind when wilt thou blow"—means more than the most deathless speech of Hamlet. But this is merely the delight in poetry's infinite variety, and there will be relationships that may be neglected but, once consummated, will never be broken.

How happy that it is not a case of either/or. There have been periods—one is now a not-very-distant memory—in which whole categories of poetry were officially discarded; categories of poetry, not of quality. One of the better facets of the present scene is the widening recognition of how feeble are the relations between category and quality. Almost on the heels of the mulish opposition to the breaking with established poetic forms came the reverse rigidity, the mind-set in which rhyme, the lyric note, or even form itself was seen as the foe of creativity. If giraffe were the animal of choice, zebra, however splendid a specimen, must put on giraffe-hood, often with labored results.

Though the present climate can change at any moment, there is a most welcome lack of the hubris of treating poetry as though it were a sort of literary dog show, in which certain breeding characteristics were required.

It seems to me that what is truly important and can scarcely be overestimated is courage in taking the high ground for a form of literature that, because it is the least widely read, may be treated as esoteric and dispensable, beyond the university. Caviar to the general reader remains caviar. And, while poetry has no right to rank itself in relation to other forms of more accessible literature, it retains its unique stature.

Lip service is widely given to this point of view, but the fact is that any art form which falls significantly short of its appropriate audience works against heavy odds. How many of us know intelligent literate people, genuinely readers, au courant with biography, history, essays, novels, who have not voluntarily read a poem since they left college?

The best in poetry makes strenuous demands upon its reader, who must be capable of absorbing the concentration he is receiving. And in the case of poetry even more is asked. Our reader is being asked to communicate in a language the *use* of which is strange to him. The words, the vowels and consonants, that have been his work force, have ordered his meals and made his appointments, composed the lines of his newspaper and bombarded him with advertisements, are now being employed in a totally other sense—Emily Dickinson's "slant" truth. It is not, as beginners often rashly assume, that there is such a thing as contemporary "poetic language." This is language that is being transformed not in its identity but in its usage. And we are back to Williams's dictum, "You have no other language for it than the poem." The words that haunt us, and have conquered a hundred or a thousand years without damage, are our own words, used in a way incomprehensible to the newspaper or the treatise. Auden remarked that a publisher would rather encounter a burglar in his office than a poet, and that Audenesque comment has within it an uncomfortable grain of truth. The publisher's reaction is far from unreasonable. He may, and probably does, assume that further relations with the poet are going to cost him money. And they are going to cost him money because of the general reaction that poetry is a fine thing, even an exalted one, but not something with which his general reader is prone to mess about.

This general perception can have desolating results, if poetry's high ground is not held. Recently, a notable literate writer suggested publicly that the literary sections of newspapers should totally eliminate reviews of poetry since no one reads them but other poets. Never mind the inaccuracy of the injunction's premise. Never mind that with bookstores reluctant to stock poetry and poets struggling with problems of practical and professional survival the columns of the better newspapers are the lifeline between them and the rare but far from nonexistent reader. This argument seems to be: if they are not widely read, let us ensure that they are less widely read. Such a statement is not going to destroy the writing or publishing of poetry. Nothing will. But it can make each more lonely a process.

The balance between hubris and respect is as delicate as it is vital. A writer who assumes great importance because of an achievement is suffering from the former. One who does not make the highest claim for the art itself is bankrupt of the latter. In the case of poetry it would be hard to overestimate its nature. Keats, suffering from every conceivable discouragement—physical, emotional, and critical—had ravaging doubts of what he had accomplished; he put that bitter doubt into his epitaph. But never for one moment did he doubt the power or significance of what he was desperately attempting. He believed that he lived, worthily or unworthily, in the company of the great. The "poets dead and gone" were his compatriots in the country of his endeavor.

There have been some shaking statements recently—a voiced assumption that the arts, and specifically poetry, need not really be taken as making any serious demand on the attention, respect, or money of the general public. That is the sort of pit into which we fall, but it is not deep or new or permanent. There is, as Tom Wolfe, for example, has pointed out in *The Bonfire of the Vanities,* a currently thriving admiration for illiteracy. We reel from too much, too fast, surface communication, which proliferates into a frenzy of quick yells, while communication at any depth goes on, like an underground river, suspect but unsuppressable.

A child, aware of something that has suffered a sea change and is now both strange and rare, may never write a word of poetry—but the need for it is there. A phrase may be a formula that works the transforming magic. The old cliché of experience, that the barbarian burns the library first, is as contemporary as the clock's hand.

If one tries for one moment truly to imagine a world in which poetry, in the deepest sense, is nonexistent—why, that is Hell, nor are we out of it. It would so rob the senses and drain the mind that one of those ashy lunar landscapes would show in comparison as fruitful. Time, which is excluded from the center of the creative process and slides harmlessly from a great poem, is the ultimate critic. One has only to look back on the rise-and-fall, shrink-and-swell process of contemporary evaluations to notice how fallible are the up-to-the-moment judgments. Names advance, recede; are covered, emerge; reveal themselves ultimately as durable, or not. All the peripheral colorings—reviews, awards, the effects of desperate or erratic or tragic or serene identities—are muted and fade, leaving perhaps a canon of work, perhaps a few lines in an anthology, perhaps an absence. The link between the survivors is the angle of a vision that is forever other than that of prose; Dickinson's slant truth, which isolates the moment from all preconceptions and from the deadly silent covering of the moss of habit—the eye's and the mind's.

The poet writing is confused by the totality of what he conceives. It is impossible for him to see clearly the poem, tinged as it is with his intentions and brutally cut off from its inception. It is Marlowe all over again: the thing lost "which into words no virtue can digest."

There is a final privacy in the act of that effort. However shared with others in the process—or however part of a working group or of a trend or a movement—the actual moment of conception is deeply private. What is seen is between the poem and the poet.

That strange ferocious, intimate encounter can no more be described than shared. All the poet can explain is that it is "As if . . . "—John Ciardi's two key words.

So I shall end with a poem, a failure as all such reports must be but the closest I can come to the matter. Some of the magic lies in the unlikeliness of locale: where on earth can it *not* be?

Lion under Maples

The lion, awake, is out there.
What is a lion doing under the maples?
The sun catches him. She knows
the calm ferocious face set

in its monstrance of
chrysanthemum shag. The eye
is golden, but too far to see.
Now there is no glimpse at all.

But she has met him before
this. And with fortune
she will. In a clearing,
in the heat, in a wink.

Then she will be left
without fear. With great power:
everything be still,
the great head lift.

From Anne to Marianne
Some Women in American Poetry

The title of this talk was selected with care. Few things are more boring than lists, and what I want to talk about in this brief time is not a chronological survey of the women poets of America. I want to look at the atmosphere in which they worked, to attempt to understand a little of its pressures and permissions; and I hope that in some mysterious way I may manage to combine elements of the involved and of the objective. As an American woman poet, I can scarcely fail to be involved, but it is the poetry, not the nationality or the sex, that finally matters. In this whole question sentimentality and exhortation are equally lethal, and there is a delicate balance between ignoring the question of power and powerlessness and making social and human problems, instead of the poetry, the center of attention.

The arts have a frequently quarrelsome, but always close, relationship. The Walters Art Gallery is currently exhibiting a show interestingly called "Old Mistresses," this being not a sort of Nell Gwynn exploration but a commentary on the ease with which we automatically accept the classification "Old Masters." What some of the passages in the Walters *Bulletin* tell us is so closely related to the history of American women who have practiced another art form, that of poetry, that I must quote it. The *Bulletin* itself quotes an influential book of etiquette of the period of Mary Cassatt, which sums up the desirable attitude for women who are in danger of becoming involved in the arts:

As the 1971–73 Consultant in Poetry, Josephine Jacobsen delivered this lecture at the Library of Congress on 1 May 1972.

To be able to do a great many things tolerably well, is of infinitely more value to a woman, than to be able to excel in any one. By the former, she may render herself generally useful; by the latter, she may dazzle for an hour. . . . So far as cleverness, learning, and knowledge are conducive to a woman's moral excellence, they are therefore desirable, and no further. All that would occupy her mind to the exclusion of better things, all that would involve her in the mazes of flattery and admiration [mazes, of course, untrod by masculine foot], all that would tend to draw away her thoughts from others and fix them on herself, ought to be avoided as an evil to her, however brilliant or attractive it may be in itself.[1]

The Walters's voice adds: "Adopting this philosophy would automatically prevent a woman, married or single, from developing a serious commitment to any profession." And it notes that after Mary Cassatt defied her father's prohibition, went to Europe, and by a tremendous struggle established herself as a serious painter—and incidentally supported herself as such—the denouement was characteristically discouraging:

Although Cassatt's father had been strictly against her sojourn in Europe, shortly after she settled in Paris he forgot his misgivings and brought the entire family to live with her.

The *Bulletin* adds that from then on she ran the household, took her invalid mother on health trips, nursed her ailing sister, and superintended the family's numerous moves, without it having seemed to occur to anyone that this was making any illegitimate inroads on her professional work or her creative energy.

This has a sadly familiar ring. Anne Bradstreet, the only poet of creative stature, with the exception of Edward Taylor, in a hundred years of American literature, was well aware of the reaction to her writing poetry at all. She wrote, with considerable bluntness, in the "The Prologue":

I am obnoxious to each carping tongue
Who says my hand a needle better fits,
A poet's pen all scorn I should thus wrong,
For such despite they cast on female wits:

If what I do prove well, it won't advance,
They'll say it's stol'n, or else it was by chance.

That is an undermining atmosphere. This reaction, of course, was not entirely limited to women. In *One Hundred American Poems* Selden Rodman quotes a letter that Herman Melville's wife wrote to her mother in 1859: "Herman has taken to writing poetry. You need not tell anyone for you know how such things get around." The distinction, however, remains in the fact that men were not supposed to write poetry because it was unsuitable, since they had things of authority and importance to do. Women were not supposed to write poetry because buttons would stay missing and meals be late, not to mention the degradation of morals.

It is simply impossible, as it is in the case of all highly subjective and emotional issues, to say with any certainty what effect the problems and harassments actually traceable to Anne Bradstreet's femininity had on her work, chilling and shrinking it: the overwhelming atmosphere of incredulity and misprision; the physical strains of a woman's life in what she described as "the savage wilderness of America," where she bore eight children and watched the deaths of three small grandchildren, two little girls, one aged a year and a half, the other three years and seven months, and a little boy who lived a month and a day. Surrounded by so much death, the old struggle to accept came through:

But plants new set to be eradicate,
And buds new blown to have so short a date,
Is by His hand alone that guides nature and fate.

And then the more desolate:

I knew she was but as a withering flower,
That's here today, perhaps gone in an hour;
Like as a bubble, or the brittle glass,
Or like a shadow turning as it was.
More fool then I to look on that was lent
As if mine own, when thus impermanent.

There is a Herrick-like echo in those lines.

In addition to the mental climate peculiar to women, there was the total lack of immediate contact with any world of letters. Kenneth Silverman, speaking in *Colonial American Poetry* of the appalling doggerel turned out, points up this barrenness:

> although there was a great volume of verse produced in the colonies, there never was a literary class. In a century and a half of their existence the colonies supported not one professional imaginative writer.[2]

It is amazing what a death grip the concept of genteel composition had. With a raw and magnificent continent surrounding them, with melodrama, conquest, cruelty, courage, and despair all around them, the colonial poets struggled to simulate the ambience of a salon. Silverman comments:

> The jarring effect of much eighteenth-century colonial verse, the reader's sense that the poet has not responded appropriately to the occasion, is the upshot of training a refined and chaste diction on the affairs of unformed towns and wilderness outposts.[3]

The women writing poetry in this entire period do seem to have been genuinely and often passionately involved in writing as a form of good works. It is a sobering instruction to see how poorly verse, widely acclaimed for its propaganda value in the interest of excellent causes, has withstood the test of time. Actually, the case for polemical poetry is put grandiloquently, but rather movingly, in Samuel Kettell's early *Specimens of American Poetry:*

> when the aim of the aggressor is at the very heart of civil liberty, the dwellers in the shades of the Academy, and even the loiterers in the laurel groves of the Muses have never been the last to repel the advances of the invader.

That is the principle. The practice has been less impressive. There was an enormous amount of poetry written by women, attacking current evils: slavery, alcoholism, the oppression of the working classes, the oppression of the Indian. Some of it, in its day, did quite probably influence other human beings and so, in some minute degree, succeed in its author's purpose. As poetry, it left scarcely a wrack behind. Lydia Huntley Sigourney wrote a just and spirited and far from untalented poem called "The Indian's Welcome to the Pilgrim Fathers." But not even our present high concern with the reevaluation of the confrontations between Indians and settlers has served to revive interest in it. In our day there are poems by Josephine Miles, Denise Levertov, and Adrienne Rich good enough to give the lie to the generalization that poetry with an object is, per se, bad poetry, but the winnowing-out has been, in the long view, usually pitiless to the poetry of polemics.

Although the poetry of colonial America was very bad indeed, its content does tell us a number of things. What were the chief elements in the attitudes of American women poets in the long desert stretching between Anne Bradstreet and Emily Dickinson? The chief elements—and this statement is less provocative than realistic—were those one might expect from a body of literate, highly privileged slaves. In general life is seen as something to be endured; emotion as something foredoomed; death as a release, even for the young. Much of the poetry of any force deals with the idea of emotional escape—as indeed, does so much of the later poetry of Emily Dickinson. In a period when, out of a family of fourteen or fifteen children, five or six might well die in infancy or early childhood, death as an omnipresent reality was a towering presence. The constants in the lives of women poets in the first hundred and fifty years on this continent were endurance, faith (often less as a conviction than as a desperate refuge), and a courage that was less ardent than fatalistic. When Louis Imogen Guiney, an uneven but much underrated poet, later wrote in "The Kings,"

> The terrible Kings are on me,
> . . . .
> Mind's Doubt and Bodily Pain,
> And pallid Thirst of the Spirit
> That is kin to the other twain, . . .

she was echoing her predecessors. Expressed agnosticism, in a woman, would have been as unseemly (and this is the point) as a talent for wrestling, so that whatever agonies of doubt the events of their lives might induce must be met and vanquished, or not, in secret.

It would be naive in the extreme to imagine that women poets accepted the innate superiority of men as mentors or artists without inner questioning, but for the most part any overt caviling took the form of the lightest of mockery. I want to read two brief verses, each of which is typical of a sort of graceful disillusionment and more than typical of its period. Hannah Parker Kimball's "One Way of Trusting":

Not trust you, dear? Nay, 't is not true.
  As sailors trust the shifting sea
From day to day, so I trust you.
  They know how smooth the sea can be;
And well they know its treachery
  When tempests blow; yet forth they trust
Their ships, as in security.
  They trust it, dear, because they must.

And Charlotte Perkins Stetson relieved her feelings after encountering the resistance of a male to the very notion of change, no matter what improvement it involved.

A Conservative

The garden beds I wandered by
  One bright and cheerful morn,
When I found a new-fledged butterfly,
  A-sitting on a thorn,
A black and crimson butterfly,
  All doleful and forlorn.

. . . .

Cried he, "My legs are thin and few
  Where once I had a swarm!
Soft fuzzy fur—a joy to view—
  Once kept my body warm,
Before these flapping wing-things grew,
  To hamper and deform!"

At that outrageous bug I shot
  The fury of mine eye;
Said I, in scorn all burning hot,
  In rage and anger high,
"You ignominious idiot!
  Those wings are made to fly!"

"I do not want to fly," said he,
  "I only want to squirm!"
And he drooped his wings dejectedly,
  But still his voice was firm:
"I do not want to be a fly!
  I want to be a worm!"

It is a gentle stricture.

I may interpolate here that there has been a strong implication by gentlemen reviewers that there is something intrinsically humorous and definitive, in the worst sense, about the three-name woman poet. And, indeed, a great number of the triple-threat ladies have been very, very bad. If, however, the poetic stature of Ralph Waldo Emerson, Edgar Allan Poe, Edwin Arlington Robinson, Gerard Manley Hopkins, or William Butler Yeats, for example, has been pegged to the number of their employed names, I have not observed it.

And it is only fair to admit that, if most early American poetry written by women was little better than refined doggerel, one can usually suffer similar shock from their male counterparts. One reads a woman's ode to General Washington and encounters the following lines:

And Echo no longer is plaintively mourning,
But laughs and is jocund as we,
And the turtle-eyed nymphs, to their cots all returning,
Carve Washington on every tree.

It takes one a minute to realize that the turtle-eyed nymphs returning to their cots do not represent a sort of reptilian dormitory but, rather, doves. But then one encounters a patriotic poem of exhortation by the author of "Dixie," Albert Pike, as he adjures his fellow Confederates,

Strong as lions, swift as eagles,
Back to their kennels hunt these beagles!

I do think the picture of a combination of lions and eagles attacking a group of beagles seems unfair.

In the long line that stretches from the bleak poetic environment of Anne Bradstreet to the complex surroundings of Marianne Moore, it is interesting, I think, to note certain resemblances between two of the finest American poets: Miss Moore herself and Emily Dickinson. Each was a spinster. Each lived uninvolved in the physical and emotional relationships that alter the daily circumstances of a wife or mother. Each had a fine quiddity that went its own way, owing nothing to the current poetic fashion. Marianne Moore, of course, lived a life enormously enriched by contacts with her peers, by access to other milieux, by her freedom from the rigid expectations of contemporaries. Emily Dickinson had a close kinship with her predecessors not only in her preoccupation with death, which Conrad Aiken so rightly noted, but in that same sense of suffocation, in the passionate need for an emotional breakthrough, which gives her work so many of its images. Three very brief Dickinson poems make, I think, an entire emotional history. I want to read them in sequence, without comment.[4]

What Soft—Cherubic Creatures—
These Gentlewomen are—
One would as soon assault a Plush—
Or violate a Star—

Such Dimity Convictions—
A Horror so refined
Of freckled Human Nature—
Of Deity—ashamed—

It's such a common—Glory—
A Fisherman's—Degree—
Redemption—Brittle Lady—
Be so—ashamed of Thee—

And the next:

Exultation is the going
Of an inland soul to sea,
Past the houses—past the headlands—
Into deep Eternity—

Bred as we, among the mountains,
Can the sailor understand
The divine intoxication
Of the first league out from land?

And the last:

How many times these low feet staggered—
Only the soldered mouth can tell—
Try—can you stir the awful rivet—
Try—can you lift the hasps of steel!

Stroke the cool forehead—hot so often—
Lift—if you care—the listless hair—
Handle the adamantine fingers
Never a thimble—more—shall wear—

Buzz the dull flies—on the chamber window—
Brave—shines the sun through the freckled pane—
Fearless—the cobweb swings from the ceiling—
Indolent Housewife—in Daisies—lain!

So little did Moore or Dickinson draw the matter of their poems from events and circumstantial changes in their own lives. Dickinson's came from within. Moore's, most of the time, from reading—reading of the odd, the particular, the out-of-the-way, the intricate. The overwhelming majority of her poems were drawn from bits of information that, like a sublime pack rat, she carried off, only to return in their place a masterly poem. There has been much recent discussion of *attention* as prayer, and William Stafford has discussed *poetry* as *attention.* Observation, raised to a certain degree, is a kind of love. Marianne Moore is the empress of observation. This is a passage from the book that William Mueller and I wrote on Samuel Beckett—we speak of Beckett's quality as poet:

> There is the poetry in which the observation is of such passionate fidelity . . . [that its intensity of] vision celebrates the nature of

> the thing observed, be that nature what it may. . . . In this intensification . . . the things of . . . poetry are seen by that peculiar clarity in which trees, flowers, a cat on green grass will stand in the light just before a thunderstorm, when the grass seems itself to give off light and the flowers to be carved on the air. The poetry consists . . . in the intensification of the thing itself.[5]

In the wonderful, casual phrase Miss Moore paid attention, and the things to which she paid it rewarded her: the jerboa, the swan, a steeplejack, a scalpel, the weasel, steam rollers, mongooses, snails, racehorses, steel, granite, giraffes, baseball, and their qualities and uses. Her attention ran below the surface: how yarn is dyed, how the structure of a wing functions, how a steeple is gilded, how an octopus kills its prey with "concentric, crushing rigor." On and on. A man's eye for the accurate detail, Anne Bradstreet's detractors would have said. But this sort of eye is notably shared by May Swenson and by Elizabeth Bishop.

The liberation by art precedes the liberation by circumstance. By the time in which an American woman, Harriet Monroe, was establishing a magazine, *Poetry,* which was to become perhaps the world's leading journal of poetry, the entire paralyzing structure of the attitude toward women writers had begun to show cracks and then gaps. In the first half of this century no one could argue that Elinor Wylie or Edna St. Vincent Millay had been forced into passive attitudes in the face of a masculine world. Yet, in the technical sense, they were still sports, and their response to life was often a sort of ricochet of their reaction to a masculine world. Millay, in particular, showed clearly a sort of midway struggle in the process of self-identification. A new note is sounded. This is not one of her best poems, but it is the perfect illustration of her simultaneous attack and insecurity:

> I, being born a woman and distressed
> By all the needs and notions of my kind,
> Am urged by your propinquity to find
> Your person fair, and feel a certain zest
> To bear your body's weight upon my breast:
> So subtly is the fume of life designed,
> To clarify the pulse and cloud the mind,
> And leave me once again undone, possessed.

Think not for this, however, the poor treason
Of my stout blood against my staggering brain,
I shall remember you with love, or season
My scorn with pity,—let me make it plain:
I find this frenzy insufficient reason
For conversation when we meet again.

That's a far cry, but it still assumes "the needs and notions" of a woman to be her Achilles' heel. The later *Conversation at Midnight* examines the conversation of six men, without hostility and with considerable empathy. It is noticeable that the only woman present is the observant spirit of Vincent, who notoriously preferred masculine company. Miss Millay had the misfortune to be too often remembered by the taglines of her light verse, her shining palaces built on the sands and her candle flaming at each end. Her reputation is now in that trough between the adulation of her work when it was in vogue and the steady respect I believe it will be entitled to, in its finest forms. I notice that Karl Shapiro has spoken of returning to his "schoolboy love Millay" and being enchanted all over again.

What of the women poets of the present? Without for a moment blinking the fact that the scales are still heavily loaded in the world of everyday activity, it would be impossible, I think, to maintain the claim that women poets today have any limitation imposed upon their concepts, or the expression of those concepts. Influences, however, can be extremely subtle and yet strong. Since the vast majority of women do not actually follow as many styles of life, move about in their environments in just the same way, experience the same physical and economic pressures as do men—to that extent the material that comes naturally to their hand is more limited. A woman who is not, in the popular imagination, responsible for the economic support of a large family, a woman who is not going to be instructed to drop a bomb or wield a bayonet, is having, for better or worse, her separate experience. How much this will change is here beyond the point. The fact is that, as Dickinson was able to pour a passionate emotional life into the tiny mold of her circumstances, it has been demonstrated again and again that, when it comes to making bricks without straw, women have possessed an infinite and mysterious skill. More and more straw becomes available. The poetry of women today does not show an overwhelming satisfaction with the quality of that straw. The poetry of Mona Van Duyn, Gwendolyn Brooks, Isabella Gardner, Adrienne Rich, Anne Sexton, Carolyn Kizer, is racked by the pressures and tensions of their wider experience. Julia Randall is one of the few who, more and more, show a quality of underlying radiance—a sort of receptive joy under the full recognition of suffering and even horror. There is a beautiful poem by Muriel Rukeyser that illustrates the sort of radiance of which I am speaking. It's called "This Place in the Ways":

> Having come to this place
> I set out once again
> On the dark and marvelous way
> From where I began:
> Belief in the love of the world,
> Woman, spirit, and man.
>
> Having failed in all things
> I enter a new age
> Seeing the old ways as toys,
> The houses of a stage
> Painted and long forgot;
> And I find love and rage.
>
> Rage for the world as it is
> But for what it may be
> More love now than last year.
> And always less self-pity
> Since I know in a clearer light
> The strength of the mystery.
>
> And at this place in the ways
> I wait for song,
> My poem-hand still, on the paper,
> All night long.
> Poems in throat and hand, asleep,
> And my storm beating strong!

I believe that the incoming tide of good poetry by American women is going to expand and deepen, not steadily—poetry never works in that way—but erratically. It is not any security on the part of women that is going to cause this to happen. Poetry has small traffic with security. What *will* contribute is the sense of the freedom, and hence power, of the individual woman (if the realization of that status for women does not tragically coincide with the diminution of all of us, men and women alike)—the right of the human being who is a woman to act, and react, *as* an individual, as the sort of human creature she is, without being first and most important judged within the context of that constricting niche to which society has assigned her.

William Jay Smith quotes Louise Bogan in his fine lecture *A Woman's Words:* "the woman poet has her singular role and precious destiny." In a preface I wrote some years ago to *Lyrics of Three Women* (one of whom was Washington's May Sullivan), I said of the best women poets: "They extract, from the husk; they mine the lode for what it yields, and learn, as they do it." Like Roethke, they learn by going where they have to go.

Power is related to energy, and poetry is energy. The power to which poetry is allied is not political or financial power, but moral, physical, and intellectual power. Bad things, such as war, suffering, and competition under harsh conditions, often produce magnificent by-products such as courage, compassion, and skilled responsibility—what Hopkins called "the achieve of, the mastery of the thing." Not only have women not had physical power analogous to that of men; it must be remembered that until this century they never had the power delegated through the machine—electricity, the automobile, the household robots that remove much of the drudgery—and that in the past, where they had native intellectual and artistic power, it was all too often cut off from implementation. No group oppressed—and it is possible to speak of oppression, since the denial to any individual of the power within her human potential is certainly the earmark of oppression—no group oppressed ever frees itself or flowers without the traces of that oppression, without a shrillness, an aggressiveness, an infatuation with its own idiosyncracies, as though anything, to be interesting or valid, had only to belong to them. I think much of that extravagantly confessional kind of poetry written by women is caused in part by the desire to assert emotional, intellectual, and physical problems without that plastic covering of reticence and euphemism that was demanded by an earlier day. I remember Auden mentioning, in a poem that catalogs the sins for which men may or may not be forgiven, the assumption that " 'Woman is naturally pure / Since she has no moustache.' "

There have been some harsh descriptions of writers as such. Kenneth Rexroth, always a fast man with a sharp word, paints a fairly gruesome picture in *American Poetry in the Twentieth Century:*

> By and large, writers are not very nice people. Most of them are quarrelsome, vindictive, malicious. There are too many piglets, and too little swill in the trough, so there is a good deal of squealing and backbiting. American writers have a fixed idea that they are not welcome in their society and this makes them arrogant.[6]

However much this seems exaggerated, or indeed distorted, no writer would deny its kernel of truth. And, if most of the best of the women poets seem curiously uninfected with the virus, it may be cynically argued that until fairly recently the trough was off limits, and they had formed a habit of doing without it. Yet I think it cause for pride that most of the good poetry being written by women has a largeness, a lack of pettiness, a reaching over barriers. To believe that the poetry of women has an especial quality is simply another way of saying that the feminine ethos has its own unique and pervasive quality to offer to the art of poetry.

The making of comparisons, of ranking, of first-, second-, and thirding of poets, is a second-rate occupation. George Garrett told me something that is beautifully relevant to this. Some members of an audience who were hostile to W. H. Auden and were sitting on the front row at his lecture asked him, in a provocative manner, whom he considered the five top poets now writing. George said that Mr. Auden bent over, peering formidably down at them, and said, "Poetry isn't—(pause)—a horse race, you know." All too often it is treated as though it were. The issue is not how many women poets will "make it" or in what order of win, place, or show. The core of the matter is the poetry; that it be written, by man or woman; that it be recognized and welcomed.

If, in the seventeenth and eighteenth centuries, it was difficult for any woman poet fully to realize her talent, for the woman who was black the difficulty approximated an impossibility. No one can estimate what poetic creativity was smothered under the weight of forced illiteracy, isolation, and the sense of hopelessness. Someone like the distinguished black woman Sojourner Truth (of whom Edmund Wilson writes in *Patriotic Gore,* and who was the heroine of a play of that name by Katherine Garrison Chapin, which ran for many weeks in Harlem) found her outlet in preaching. She was musical and eloquent; inevitably, she functioned in the ways open to her, as singer, as evangelist. But at last the poetry of black women is beginning to come into its own.

Can one say that now, in this period roughly coinciding with the end of Marianne Moore's career, there is a definite shape, a direction, an overriding pattern, as legacy in the work of American women poets? Definitely, one cannot.

Sylvia Plath's tragic, inward-turned work; Elizabeth Bishop's and May Swenson's marvelous observation and justice; Louise Bogan's real majesty; Isabella Gardner's highly charged and witty work, with its kinship to Millay; Josephine Miles's and Adrienne Rich's socially oriented work; Anne Sexton's passionate and dramatic self-analysis; June Jordan's racial concern; Julia Randall's lyric and metaphysical radiance; Carolyn Kizer's cool, satiric, and highly feminine work—all have little to indicate to us of any future "trend." Interestingly enough, there does not seem to have been a great deal of acute interest in the more far-out forms of technical innovation among the majority of these poets. Never for a minute did they feel that the rupturing of form and structure alone could produce originality, nor did they lose sight of the fact that shock, and the recognition of its validity, come about organically, within the poem.

There is here freedom from the restriction of imposed assumptions. These poets have rejected limitation of subject matter, of vocabulary, of viewpoint. Little of their work is cast in traditional form; rather, form is beautifully responsive to the needs of the individual poem. It is, much of it, distinguished poetry, and in my opinion it holds its own in quality, if not quantity, with poetry now being written by American men. But what a meaningless comparison, basically, that is. Once the poem is released, how little the poet owns it or, indeed, matters to the poem. The poem has always been injured by the poet. Never, by man or woman, has it been fully released to its potential. Christopher Marlowe spoke for every poet when he wrote long ago in "Tamburlaine the Great" (and this is my favorite statement of what happens to a poem between its conception and its execution):

> If all the pens that ever poets held,
> Had fed the feeling of their masters' thoughts,
> And every sweetness that inspir'd their hearts,
> Their minds, and muses on admired themes:
> If all the heavenly quintessence they still
> From their immortal flowers of poesy,
> Wherein, as in a mirror, we perceive
> The highest reaches of a human wit:
> If these had made one poem's period,
> And all combin'd in beauty's worthiness,
> Yet should there hover in their restless heads
> One thought, one grace, one wonder, at the least,
> Which into words no virtue can digest . . .

Always, the struggle is to help the poem release itself from the things it cannot, in various stages, do without: publishers, editors, critics, funds, sponsors. Always the effort must be to shift the emphasis back to where it belongs, to the poem, which, though injured and subjected to the thousand ills that print is heir to, must escape and survive.

I have been speaking tonight as a poet and a woman. I would like to end by reading a poem about that freedom of the poem itself from being anyone's possession, about that marvelous thing, escaped, which, since it belongs to no one, speaks to its own. That is what is left in the end.

The Poem Itself

> From the ripe silence it exploded silently.
> When the bright debris subsided
> it was there.

Invisible, inaudible; only
the inky shapes betrayed it.
Betrayed, is the word.

Thence it moved into squalor,
a royal virgin in a brothel,
improbably whole.

It had its followers, pimps, even
its lovers. The man responsible
died, eventually.

When the dust of his brain left the bones
the bond snapped. It escaped to itself.
It no longer answered.

On the shelf, by the clock's tick, in the black
stacks of midnight: it is. A moon
to all its tides.

NOTES

1. Mrs. [Sarah S.] Ellis, *The Family Monitor and Domestic Guide* (New York; H. G. Langley, 1844); quoted in Ann Gabhert and Elizabeth Broun, "Old Mistresses: Women Artists of the Past," *Bulletin of the Walters Art Gallery* 24 (April 1972).

2. Kenneth Silverman, ed., *Colonial American Poetry* (New York: Hafner Publishing Company, 1968), 4.

3. Ibid., 7.

4. These three Dickinson poems are taken from *The Complete Poems of Emily Dickinson,* ed. Thomas H. Johnson (Boston: Little, Brown, 1960).

5. Josephine Jacobsen and William R. Mueller, *The Testament of Samuel Beckett* (New York: Hill and Wang, 1964), 35, 38.

6. Kenneth Rexroth, *American Poetry in the Twentieth Century* (New York: Herder and Herder, 1971), 84.

The Instant of Knowing

When I thought about this talk, I thought that tonight was the night on which I wanted to say whatever I knew about the nature of poetry; not the sum of what I know (whatever that may be) but its essence. The dangers attendant on being a poet and the dangers attendant on being Poetry Consultant are obviously close kin. I am neither so impertinent nor so naive as to work toward the definition of poetry, but I want to end tonight by telling a story, a true story, which implies as much of a definition as I have come by.

What seems to me the chief danger of the profession and of the job? A veering, a built-in tendency to jib—that perpetual tendency to veer from the core of the job, the core of the profession; that response to time and distraction pressures, or to attraction, which shakes the magnetic needle off center.

As I see it, the cause, the purpose, and the end of the position of Consultant in Poetry is poetry itself, as poetry itself is the poet's own job. There are so many good things that hover on the periphery: the setting, the methods, the supportive structure, human relations, social relations, the hope for lack of pomposity, availability to genuine need, the mastering of the shapes of time and effort. The center of everything is the poem. Nothing is important in comparison to that. Anything that in some valid way is not directly connected with that current of energy that is the poem is dispensable.

In the poet's own world the distracting forces multiply. The poet, if he is a publishing professional, is instantly immersed in the morass of acceptance, rejection, publication, rankings, sales,

---

A lecture delivered at the Library of Congress on 7 May 1973.

status, lectures, readings. (And here I'm leaving quite out of consideration the whole academic scene in which most poets earn their livings in ways often only marginally connected with the actual process of writing poems.) And sometimes it is as pathetic as it is alarming to see, in individual cases, how these considerations come to take on proportionately more importance than the poem itself. Sometimes, indeed, a scene degenerates into the metaphor of a bargain counter sale where perspiring aspirants paw and grope for the bargain of success.

The Muse of poetry is a very fierce Muse indeed. I think of Stevens's image of the poem: "The lion sleeps in the sun. Its nose is on its paws. It can kill a man." That ferocity is more easily aroused by posturing, by hubris, than even by ineptitude, though in milder moments it does eat ineptitude alive. I wrote a few weeks ago a poem that I preferred to leave alone but which nagged me until it was written. It posited a group of self-admiring and mutually congratulatory poets, reading to one another in an ecstasy of false sensitivity that would rival that of Mme. Verdurin, who are visited by the Muse whom they had lightly invoked.

The Poetry Consultant is dogged by the danger appropriate to each attempt. Is he or she tempted by the exhilaration of uncovering talent? Splendid. A flood washes all away. The only generalization in which I now totally believe is that every human creature in the United States of America writes—or has a friend, lover, or relative who writes—poetry. Does he or she give an interview? From far and near arrive touching and infuriating letters, explaining that ever since seeing the consultant's face reproduced in their local press (here they enclose a dim copy, indistinguishable as to sex or features), the undersigned knew at once that the consultant was tenderhearted, acute, compassionate, and active, living only to aid writers economically distressed and aesthetically bypassed by a callous public. Does the consultant appear upon the stage, introducing a poet or poets? Letters rain like hail from other unpresented poets.

But these pressures, compared to the possibilities inherent in the job, are minor. There are graver pressures attendant on the act of poetry itself. Perhaps the gravest is the burden of the word as medium; the word in relation to paint or notes or marble.

The word with its connotations. The word, above all, with its definitions. The word frayed, debased, exploited, disfigured, and, most formidably of all, trapped in its dictionary. This is a challenge unequaled in any other art. John Ashbery, in his curriculum vitae when *The Tennis Court Oath* was published, elucidated the whole problem. He wrote: "What I like about music is its ability of being convincing, of carrying an argument through successfully to the finish, though the terms of this argument remain unknown quantities." Poetry makes its argument, to a lesser or greater degree, with the terms stated. Poetry names. If there is one thing it does, it is to name. It imposes identity. And it must name with words. John Barth, in one of his beautiful explosions, says this of the words with which the writer deals: "words . . . as they come, or long since came: once-living creatures caught and fossiled in the clay; bones displaced by alien mineral, grown with crystals, hued with the oxides of old corrosion, heaved and worn and rearranged by the eons' ebb; shards; disjecta membra, from which the sleeping dragon is ever harder to infer."

And still the poet uses them to name. I would like to borrow a poem from my successor, Daniel Hoffman, which talks marvelously about this.

In the Beginning

On the jetty, our fingers shading
incandescent sky and sea,

my daughter stands with me.
"Boat! Boat!" she cries, her voice

in the current of speech
cascading with recognition's joys.

"Boat!" she cries; in spindrift
bobbling sails diminish,

but Kate's a joyous spendthrift
of her language's resources.

Her ecstasy's contagion
touches the whirling gulls

and turns their gibbering calls
to "Boat! Boat!" Her passion

to name the nameless pulls her
from the syllabic sea.

She points beyond the jetty
where the uncontested sun

wimples the wakeless water
and cries, "Boat!" though there is none.

But that makes no difference to Katy,
atingle with vision and word;

and why do I doubt that the harbor,
in the inner design of truth,

is speckled with tops'ls and spinnakers,
creased with the hulls of sloops?

Kate's word names the vision
that's hers; I try to share.

That verbal imagination
I've envied, and long wished for:

the world without description
is vast and wild as death;

the word the tongue has spoken
creates the world and truth.

Child, magician, poet
by incantation rule;

their frenzy's spell unbroken
defines the topgallant soul.

The naming of things, which is the poet's function, is not, like a science, progressive. It is circular, and each passage of the circle is unique. The process will also be, to whatever degree, a record of failure. There will be good poetry, and poorer poetry, and bad poetry, or, rather, stuff which is ersatz, which is not poetry at all. I have quoted before Auden's comment "Poetry is not a horse race," and the difference between the poem the poet felt within his grasp when he began to translate it into writing and the poem he finally has on paper is so much sharper and more bitter than the difference between his written poem and a lesser poem that no one can be said to have won. Anthony McNeill, the young Jamaican poet who read at the Library's conference on teaching creative writing, said that perhaps the way in which a true poet is known is by his own sense of failure.

Great poems are innocent of neither ideas nor technique. But poetry that becomes ideas or techniques has diluted to the danger point the process of poetry. As a poet advances in sophistication and technique, this danger dogs him.

Often the poet brings back very little from the instant of knowing. Sometimes, rarely, he brings back something that combines two worlds: something germane to what Yeats called "the artifice of eternity"—the made and the eternal. Such poetry may wear any mode: the august, the raucous, the witty, the tragic. Nothing could matter less. Poetry is energy, and it is poetic energy that is the source of that instant of knowing that the poet tries to name. The test for the true poetic energy that rouses Barth's sleeping dragon is, it seems to me, the only universal test that can be applied to poetry.

In the process of naming things, the poet is caught at once in the problem of naming his own time, the problem of what was called "relevancy" until that word's exhaustion gave everyone empathetic fatigue. In naming his own time, the poet may be one of those rare writers who reach community in a working solitude, though seldom in a personal one. Ionesco writes: "For solitude is not *separation* but *meditation,* and we know that social groups . . . are most often a collection of solitary human beings. No one ever talked of incommunicability at a time when men were able to isolate themselves; incommunicability and isolation are paradoxically the tragic themes of the modern world, where everything is done collectively." Ionesco asserts repeatedly that his urge toward solitude is caused by his deeply held belief that it is in their reflective solitude that men are most closely united. For the solitary writers the group experience in the pursuit of their own work is a negative experience. They work alone; the poem's inception and execution is as secret as a film's development in a darkroom. They learn, ravenously, from their fellows, their betters, the great dead, their own guts; from talk, from print, by osmosis; but they are not, and can never be, group members. Most poets, on the other hand, as John Ciardi pointed out, at some phase of their working life as poets, have been part of a group, and these have the stimulation and reinforcement that fly like sparks from the contact with congenial minds with the same general approach, objectives, and dislikes. But groups can also generate *groupthink*—that curious amalgam that bounces back and forth, carrying always some measure of other-directed debris.

This, in its totality, isn't apt to apply to a group of poets, but neither is it irrelevant. The kind of conformity that sometimes waylays the poet is almost never—indeed, I can say never—conformity to the acknowledged and enormous pressures on the general public. The general public isn't, really, a reading public by nature, and the reading public isn't, really, a poetry-reading public. Nonconformism to the advertising mind is second nature to the poet. The danger for the poet from conformism comes from within the group or even within the poetic community. It is not hard for the poet to run counter to uninformed pressure; it is sometimes very hard indeed to hold a course that may temporarily steer him counter to the informal pressure of his peers' direction, though from time to time he may find himself under the necessity to do just that. His own demon has got to say yes; after all the humility and openness and gratitude, it is his own demon that must speak. If he has connected with the source of energy, his poetry will be alive and intimately related to the most distant truth; if not, it is born dead, though it be as factually relevant as today's headlines.

The brief story I want to tell is completely concerned with that energy and how it travels and the mysterious fact that certain words, in a certain arrangement and with a certain cadence, start up a chain reaction explained by nothing in the words themselves or in their content.

An interesting argument took place last Saturday, after I had spoken at the University of Maryland. After the speech there was a panel discussion, and quite a hot controversy arose as to what degree of analysis of a poem is possible without destroying the life of the poem. A number of teachers in the audience felt that poems could be, and were, dismembered to the point of death on the operating table. Others held out, very stoutly indeed, for the belief that the more you studied the poem the more it meant to you. I understand very well the first point of view, having some years ago had a class for teachers of poetry who had been so disheartened by the poetry analysis to which they themselves had been subjected as students that they cordially disliked poetry and were now trying to learn to reapproach it, for the sake of their students and of themselves. On the other hand, it is obviously impossible to denigrate the joy and comprehension that come from a close textual reading. It seems to me that the solution of the basic problem—as Robert Frost has pointed out—lies in acknowledging as the most important element that point of mystery that is the core of the poem, that untranslatable quasar that can never fully be put into the prose of exposition. Certain words, in a certain cadence.

"Ah sun-flower! weary of time, who countes the steps of the Sun." It would be impossible to find simpler or more daily words. Or "I have been one acquainted with the night." It is something that is not music and is not talk and is both; but what it does, every single time, is touch the nerve that knows. It is, literally, an instant of knowing—of something simultaneously strange and familiar; something already known but now discovered. (That wonderful word: *dis-covered.*)

Almost thirty years ago, on a rather cold autumn afternoon, my husband and I were exploring some of the small side roads in the northern mountains of New Hampshire. One such road went over the crest of a hill and past a small and thoroughly overgrown cemetery, which obviously hadn't been used in the past decade. We stopped the car and got out and started wandering around in the tall grass, reading some of the tombstones. Some of them were tilted at angles, and some had lost letters to the weather. They said all the usual things—"Beloved wife of . . ." "He giveth his beloved rest . . ." A few said "Infant Son" or "Infant Daughter," and there were quite a lot of children. It was cold in the wind, and we started back to our car. Just before we got to the gate, which was rusted and rather lopsided, I saw a carving of a pair of clasped hands, on a leaning stone, and stooped down to look at the inscription. There was a woman's name but no relationship, and under the name and the date were carved two lines of poetry. They said:

> It is a fearful thing to love
> What Death can touch.

Eleven words, ten of them monosyllables. Immediately I thought, I know those lines; but I didn't, in the sense of placing them, and neither did my husband, though he had had exactly the same sense of recognition. They hung in my mind as though every hour they were going to place themselves. I quoted them a few times to people I thought might recognize them; always there was the same reaction: "Yes, I know that . . ." But no one did.

A few months later I wrote a longish and unsatisfactory poem about a wartime cemetery, and in it I quoted the epitaph from the tombstone. The poem was published in the *Junior League Magazine*—a periodical over which I doubt poets tended to hang. Later, I forgot about the poem, and I never included it in a book. But I didn't forget the two lines I did not write; they were there.

About four or five years later, after an illness, I came home from the hospital and found some piled-up issues of *Commonweal.* Leafing through them, I noticed a review of a play that had just opened in New York by a poet whose work had interested me when I saw his Pulitzer Prize–winning play, *Hogan's Goat.* The poet was William Alfred, and the verse-play under review was his *Agamemnon.* The review, a very favorable one, after praising the poetry and the stature of the play, went on to say that the play reached its climax in Cassandra's cry, "It is a fearful thing to love what death can touch."

I don't think I have ever had such an eerie sensation. I kept reading the words over, waiting for them to change in some particular. Then I sat down, in a sort of superstitious panic, and wrote a letter to William Alfred and asked him where he had gotten those two lines, as I had a special reason for wanting to know. He wrote back at once to say that evidently the copy of the published play that he had sent me hadn't arrived. It came in the next day, and there was a note in the front that said that Cassandra's cry, "It is a fearful thing to love what death can touch," was from a poem by Josephine Jacobsen and had been quoted to him by C. Page Smith, the historian.

A few weeks ago, when I was preparing this lecture, I did what I have waited all these years to do—I wrote to William Alfred and asked him what, exactly, he remembered. This is what he wrote me, as new to me then as it is to you tonight:

> It was Columbus Day, 1950. C. Page Smith had arranged a trip under the aegis of Samuel Eliot Morison, to Plymouth, to look at where the *Mayflower* had first landed. Professor Morison had recently lost his wife. Part of the tour, on that gray cold day, was the graveyard . . . of the pilgrims, on a small hill above the harbor. As we looked out over the sea from that rise, Page told Professor Morison of that poem of yours and of the New Hampshire tombstone . . . it haunted me as it haunts me still.

Those eleven words, put together by an unknown human being, carved by someone's hand on a grassed-over tombstone, in a deserted New Hampshire graveyard, had struck—in a chain of energy, unbelievable but natural—into my mind, then into my poem; had extricated themselves from that inferior substance and struck through the mind of another writer so forcefully that he had been compelled to speak them, to a poet-dramatist, who put them at the core of the poem that was his play; and the reviewer found them rising from that play to arrest him and put them, as the play's climax, onto the page of a magazine, later held by the person who had received their impact from the stone in the grass in the graveyard.

I think that the whole meaning of the instant of knowing lies in that circuit. A knowledge of what we already knew become for an instant so devastatingly fresh that it could be contained no more than a flash of lightning. The arrangement of the oldest human fact into certain special sounds, in a certain sequence. It is the thing that cannot be argued with. And I have always felt almost superstitious about the story, because it is such a complete one; it is, to me, of the essence of poetry. Whenever I hear someone trying to define poetry or hear myself working toward a definition, I think of that carved stone sending out its terrible energy to that nerve of knowledge in the hearer, the reader, which transmits it.

This is the live energy that keeps the mass from corruption: the venal poet who writes, the editor who publishes, the critic who analyzes, the reader who reads. What that energy speaks to is our knowledge but a dormant, denied-by-habit knowledge that is kindled to response in the rare instant.

That energy is the common quality that brings poets together: the well-known poets who walk into the Poetry Office from all over the world, the young poets who are just beginning to be sure of what they know, the Poetry Consultants who have been so different from one another but conveyors of this poetic energy. It is the kind of energy that burns away the debris. The Muse is not fond of decoration. The speech of a poet changes radically as time passes, just as the poet changes; if not, some life has died.

To end I am going to read two poems about that energy, about its lethal hostility to the ornamental or the simulated. One, a very early poem that I wrote many years ago, and one, a poem I wrote a few weeks ago. But I am going to read them in reverse order, because what I am interested in showing is not a development in one poet. What I want to show is that, though the mode of expression has changed (I certainly hope), the direction was always the same; that the poem's arc comes back to the same source.

The first poem I'm going to read actually frightened me when I wrote it. It had been a sort of jest, a laughing at, mostly, myself, in an uncongenial scene familiar to every professional poet. But then I felt that I had raised a Fury. This poem is called "When the Five Prominent Poets":

When the five prominent poets
gathered in inter-admiration
in a small hotel room, to listen
to each other, like Mme. Verdurin
made ill by ecstasy,
they dropped the Muse's name.
Who came.

It was awful.
The door in shivers, and a path
plowed like a twister through everything.
Eyeballs and fingers littered that room.
The floor exploded and the ceiling parted
and the Muse went on and up; and not a sound
came from the savage carpet.

The second poem is a very early and highly unsophisticated poem, and what interests me in reading it here is the persistence of the same conviction that the instant of knowing is undeniable, terrifying, and permanent.

Poet, When You Rhyme

Poet, when you rhyme lightly,
Do you perceive or not
The poison that steeps brightly
Your quick and fertile plot—
And brings the inward rot?

Cut back, cut back, the early,
The feebly-blooded shoot;
The knife is sharp and surly,
But cousin to the fruit,
Cut backward to the root.

Then from the vestige broken
And hacked and without leaf
On living's tiniest token,
Upon some night of grief
Will bloom the strong relief,

And toward this consummation,
By thrift and silence fed,
A man in desolation,
With you five centuries dead,
Will turn, and raise his head.

One Poet's Poetry

Until today, I have never given a lecture that was primarily concerned with the writing of my own poetry. If one's basic subject is that marvelous and terrifying procedure, the production of a poem, how in all honesty does one approach that subject?

When I was asked to talk about the writing of poetry, as seen in what I have experienced in the writing of my own, I felt in a way helpless. It is like being asked to describe oneself as alive: heart, yes; brain; body; but what incredible complexity and detail, if the picture were anywhere near complete.

Then I realized that all that could possibly be done was to say something about some of the key things that happened when one poet wrote her poetry.

I have always marveled at the cartoonist's ability to draw three lines and, by them, represent Linus's complete mental and emotional state vis-à-vis Lucy; or, for that matter, one of those pen strokes of a sketch by Matisse, pure as creation, which defines a human profile.

No one has ever totally defined the process of writing a poem or the nature of the poem itself when it has been written. But I *can* talk a little of what I myself have experienced.

First, I want to say a word or two about the deceptive medium in which the young poet is dealing. It is not necessary, or even customary, for every human being, in the course of his or her life, to put paint on canvas, or chisel stone, or finger the stops of a violin. But it is necessary and customary for the human being to

---

A lecture delivered at Agnes Scott Writers' Festival on 2 May 1975 and subsequently printed as a pamphlet by Agnes Scott College.

use words for every conceivable purpose; they are the medium in which we order our food, complain to our doctor, express our loves or animosities, ad infinitum. It would never occur to a painter or a musician or a sculptor—or, for that matter, to a figure skater or baseball pitcher—that what he or she is doing is not a special thing, requiring special tools, special training, and dominated by guidelines, acquired and self-imposed. But, since words are everybody's medium, the beginning poet often feels that there is no mysterious and unmastered field in which to step when words are put on paper. And this fact, in itself, accounts for most of the very bad poetry that is written. Words as *used* in poetry—not the words, their use—are as different from words used in prose as is the motion of a pitcher from that of a sculptor. There is no overstepping the work, the grueling, endless, so often disheartening work, though it is a truism that no amount of work alone can make an artist. The work lies in the deep rift between conception and delivery, one that, in reality, is never totally bridged.

Most poets begin to write when they are very young. I was ten when my first poem was published. And, by some awful law of diminishing returns, nothing of mine since then has appeared to me so gorgeous, so desirable, so satisfying, as those words, incarnate on the page. Because, at that time, I believed that they belonged to me. I had created them, and, like God, I saw what I had done, and it was good.

For many years after that, poetry for me was necessarily a hole-and-corner affair, fitted into the crannies of an otherwise occupied life—never abandoned, never able to take its place at the center. Then, about fifteen years ago, I came to a period in which I could work. Though I wrote and published a great deal of poetry before that time, only then did I have the opportunity to see where I was, to guess where I might be going.

A poem begins in the impulse to tell yourself something that has happened that cannot be communicated in prose.

I knew that, in attempting this particular talk, in discussing the guides that a poet, beginning to write, sets herself and how later a professional poet works, the result would be highly personal and necessarily limited to my own convictions, attempts, and experience—hence my title. And for this reason, I want to disclaim in advance any suggestion of definitive edict, and to emphasize that the obviously subjective nature of what I am going to say is due to the fact that I will be speaking as one woman, one poet, of what has happened to me in the process of practicing my profession—as Eliot austerely called the job—amid the failures, partial successes, pratfalls, and exhilaration of that harrowing metier.

Of course, there are the general rules: never assume anything to have interest as a poem because it deals with something that has happened to you. Never attempt anything that *hasn't* intense personal interest for you, simply because it seems a good subject at that time or place. Poetry is arbitrary. The logic, however brilliant and perceptive, that carries you through prose can never produce one line of poetry. The essence of poetry is the unique view—the unguessed relationship, suddenly manifest. Poetry's eye is always aslant, oblique; miniaturizing the enormous, zeroing in on the minute, vital detail until it fills the sky. And of all its hideously difficult aspects, the very most difficult is this combination: the necessity for the absolutely discovered; the necessity for the absolutely accurate. This is the accuracy of poetry, irrelevant to the accuracy of prose, and infinitely more difficult.

If the discovered relationship startles, it is because it is a real relationship. It is difficult to be hit by that arrow of revelation, but a self-inflicted, papier-mâché arrow is the worst of all. It is easy to compare a garbage can to a galaxy, but, unless you can shout, "Yes, yes," you are worse off than before. There is a line in a poem that reads, "poor Greece / the color of my old sneakers." This is a fine example of the dangers of strain. First, it hits you in the eye: imagine, comparing Greece to the color of old sneakers! Then, there is a certain excitement. It has a nice, loose motion, and there *is* a yellowed, mellow, honey-on-white look to the great stones of Greece under the Greek sun. There *is* a possible relationship between clay-mellowed white sneakers and that sun-stained white of Grecian stones. But now what have you got? You've got a simile that first wrenches your sense of reality then forces you (and the keyword is *forces*) to admit a relationship; finally, there is a lack of live fusion, which causes you to snap back into aesthetic disbelief. The conception is still-born. You are left with a failure. The relationship is too fleeting, too shallow, too cute, to take the obvious strain, and there it is, dead. The poet has gambled on it, and, after the first faint flash, it doesn't work.

This strain is, I think, the luckless characteristic, the enemy, of so much experimental verse—and, without constant and real experiment, we are all dead poets.

You have, then, these three ominous layers: the necessity for true originality; the necessity for true relationship; and the necessity for scale and tone. If you aren't let down by one, it's a marvel if you aren't by another.

What this means, basically, is that you are confronted with a terrible kind of honesty and, at the same time, held on target. It is not enough that you have felt it, though feel it you must. It is not enough, ever, that you have "an idea." There is a queasy flood of contrived poetry: poetry built out of the idea for a poem, an explanation of how the idea works, what it means. These are dead ducks; no flight. In my final lecture at the Library of Congress I used a splendid phrase of Richard Eberhart: "the instant of knowing." That is beautifully just. It *is* an instant: a word's or emotion's or event's sudden shock, which illuminates. And what it illuminates is the poet's own knowledge, your own actual knowledge of something you never knew you knew. You won't feel that the poem is "about" something. It *is* something that already exists and which you must release into its own operative force and form. The amazing thing is that the preoccupation, the images, the words themselves, can be so strong that you cannot think of them in terms of "subject matter."

When my *New and Selected Poems* came out recently, reviewer after reviewer fastened on my feeling for the wild, an empathy with the primitive, or with animal life. "*Animals?*" I said to myself. In general I dislike poems about pets. I have, growingly, a sense of annoyance and even repulsion for the arrogance of an increasingly urban human world, in which the dog, the cat, the policeman's horse, and the zoo represent all the immense, mysterious, busy, analphabetic life teeming on this planet. But it would never occur to me that I wrote poems "about animals." So I sat down one day recently and made a list of nonhuman life form in my own poetry. I came up with a partial list: crab, gorilla, cock, buffalo, mongoose, wild parrot, hyena, hummingbird, giraffe, elephant, spider, hippopotamus, crocodile, bat, starfish, reindeer, lion, wild duck, tiger, toad, leopard, turtle, bear, lizard, wolf, raccoon.

I discovered that I had, completely unconsciously, stayed away from the eagle, the lark, the hawk, and the cardinal—not because any form of life can ever be exhausted for the poet but because my own sense of them had been deadened by repetition. I have never written a poem that is basically a description of an animal. Though, again to show that no generalization whatsoever always obtains, one need only think of the brilliant descriptions of animals or fish written, for example, by Marianne Moore or Elizabeth Bishop. But these poems are far more, of course, than description, however brilliant.

There are certain aspects of poetry in which each poet feels personally uneasy, but this says little of the validity of the aspect itself. I, for example, am wary of the literary or aesthetic allusion. As far as I know, I have overtly used it in two poems—a reference to Molly Bloom and one to Mme. Verdurin. This is probably because my own reflex to such allusions is partly that they are apt to inject a secondhand experience into the poem, and partly that they assume a sort of literary collaboration on the part of the reader, something I don't in general want a poem to demand—though, oddly, in prose it gives me great pleasure to do so and to have this done to me as reader. For me the poem must have a direct, visceral effect, and I don't want the reader to have to say, "O yes, that aesthetic hypocrite, Mme. Verdurin, who gave the strained and false soirees." Yet consider what has been done in this referential vein by, for instance, Pound, Eliot, and Auden.

So—the poem will make a discovery: it will be a discovery that *moves;* it will be a discovery that has found its own body. Words become lost, over a period of time, in the crust of habitual use. I am being constantly stopped short by the resurrection of a word, by seeing it suddenly rise in its simplest and most original meaning. I remember being suddenly hit by the word *dis-cover,* by the second syllable, which hides, encrusts, shelters, and the first syllable, which rips off that shelter. It's really a rather terrifying word: the cover ripped off, and there is the hidden thing itself. But even more lost is the word *moving.* We poets often write easily, if sincerely, to each other that a poem, a line, is "moving." But what that word truly does is take us from one place to another. It is not we who have moved ourselves; that is normal and unfrightening. We have *been* moved; picked up, without our own volition, from there, and set down, here. Some change, however minute or unmeasurable, has occurred.

You remember Rilke's poem on the torso of Apollo. The poem deals entirely with the fragment of sculpture; there is no hint of a moral or ethical judgment. Then, without warning, without the slightest forced connection, comes the last line: "You must change your life." The sight has moved the viewer, involuntarily, from a contemplation, to the necessity for a voluntary change. So *discover* and *moving,* two of the encrusted words, freed, help to define the nature of a poem. A poem must *discover.* It must move the reader from the spot where it found him to the spot where he stands.

If all this makes the writing of a poem seem threateningly difficult, I am glad. A poem, once truly alive, will come out. There is no stopping it: and the more that is understood of the difficulty of freeing it, the less it will be injured in the process. I *understand* that difficulty; I never think of it when I am writing the poem; then the encounter must be free, unfearful, risky. It is only later that such understanding helps you to see what you have done and failed to do.

And here a word for the failed poem, that class that includes the massive majority of all poems conceived. Roethke has a marvelous line—"what slips away, provides." Every poet is aware of what he has learned from his own failed or fugitive poems; more, perhaps, than from any other literary experience. How often something misused, abandoned, returns, in clarity and authority, for later use elsewhere.

There are, really, extremely few themes for poems, whatever the proliferation of subjects. The themes are loneliness, love, fear, hate, beauty, death. Almost any poem worth reading has one of these threads in its texture, though its immediate subject may seem totally remote from them. But different poets come to the same theme from every conceivable angle, and the same poet approaches a theme instinctively in different ways in different stages of her development. She will suddenly find, after writing the poem without the slightest thought of its being a congener of another of her poems, that the underlying impulse is the same, taking shape quite differently; freely, without similarity, and sometimes in an opposing spirit, the other side of the coin. This is the basic richness of poetry, and, since it seems to me of acute importance, I want to get down to the process itself, by discussing three specific poems.

The poems that I have selected have a basic impulse and theme that is identical, but they are so different that they represent diverse emotional and poetic approaches.

I want to read the poems and say a word about each. First, a very early one, like the opening note of a lifelong preoccupation:

In Isolation

When at a desperate plight
His sentience quits its mesh
To taste the acrid fright
Within the alien flesh,

To know the separate pain
Which is no piece of his,
Almost a man may gain
Identity in this.

Almost he may believe
He has worked miracle
And does in fact conceive
An unfamiliar hell;

Almost he shall descry
The small and dreadful day
From which he cannot fly
Because there is no way:

Almost he has escaped
Ego's lonely law;
Here are two halves, twin-shaped,
Divided by a straw.

Just at identity,
Just at the perfect tone,
Suddenly he is free—
Suddenly it is lost . . . gone.

Once more descends the chill
The healthy life has shunned
Where move in secret still
The sad and moribund.

From artificial care
Fostered beyond its scope,
Goes up the stranger's prayer,
The insulated hope.

This poem is a head-on look at loneliness. It is loneliness seen by the nonlonely, insofar as any human is nonlonely. True identification with the overwhelmingly lonely, the lonely of dread, loss, doom, is the most fugitive identification, and the fugitive quality of the empathy is the point on which the poem turns.

The second poem deals with a discovery within the discovery of loneliness:

Deaf-Mutes at the Ballgame

In the hot sun and dazzle of grass
The wind of noise is men's voices:

A torrent of tone, a simmer of roar,
And bats crack, bags break, flags follow themselves.

The hawkers sweat and gleam in the wind of noise,
The tools of ignorance crouch and give the sign.

The deaf-mutes sit in the hurricane's eye,
The shell-shape ear and the useless tongue

Present, but the frantic fingers' pounce and bite
Is sound received and uttered.

If they blink their lids—then the whole gaudy circle
With its green heart and ritual figures

Is suddenly not: leaving two animal-quick
Wince-eyed things alone; with masses and masses

And masses of rows of seats of men
Who move their lips and listen.

While secret secret sits inside
Each, his deaf-mute, fingerless.

The discovery, the poem within a poem, has to come in two lines, as opposed to the previous sixteen; a shaft of pure isolation that is universal. There is no finger language, or tongue, that can communicate the innermost word that wishes to be spoken. The impact of those two lines must be brief and hard; six of the ten words are monosyllables. And the single last word is the shift of the whole poem's locus, right past usual pity, below and beyond it.

The final poem comes in a circle back to the first but is its opposite. This is the private, ultimate crisis but seen from *within* its total isolation. I care about this poem because in it I have done, to some extent, what I wished to do; to see visual, sensual action that, in its own field and with no overt relationship to me, tells me the thing I want to know about myself and links that to a common predicament.

The Matadors

The dirty money and the sleazy hearts
swell the *fiesta brava;*
in cheap *sol,* dear *sombra,* sit the greedy
strong-armed with expendable cokes and cushions—
missile-rebukes of buyers to the bought:

pig-eyed, big-assed, the princes of peseta,
tycoon of horses, tycoon of *billetes,*
knowers of the greasy ropes, the skid;
aficionados of the tide that turns:

the bloodshock of the trumpets,
the celestial suit, the very sand
under the sole of the slipper
crying, what is sold a man
if he loses his profit?

Yet it is silly to say
that their blood and their wrists have not spoken,
the fighters with names like lights:
El Espartaro, Manolete, Josalito.
They speak to us.

The bulls were always there;
in the moonlight pastures,
moving through the shadows
the blacker shadows.

They speak,
the matadors. To us.
Right-thinking cannot hush
them, nor the crowds, their enemy;
nor the gentle wish.

They will speak and we will answer.
Unless someone is born
who has not set himself
before the dark horned shape

alone,
set his feet in sand
calling softly, hoarsely,
Toro, toro! Venga!

In ending, I want to undercut my own conclusions to this extent: if there is a poem within, trying to emerge, and by nature it seems to be one that negates every rule of poetry, every insight gained, write it. Do not be afraid of it. Not one statement ever made about poetry can stand in the way of a true poem that violates all statements. There is no limiting the intimate relationship between poem and poet, poem and reader.

And since this talk has been necessarily such a personal one I want to end it by reading a very short poem about that last great relationship, that terrifying moment, the reading of a great poem.

Gentle Reader

Late in the night when I should be asleep
under the city stars in a small room
I read a poet. A poet: not
a versifier. Not a hot-shot
ethic-monger, laying about
him; not a diary of lying
about in cruel, cruel beds, crying.
A poet, dangerous and steep.

O God, it peels me, juices me like a press;
this poetry drinks me, eats me, gut and marrow
until I exist in its jester's sorrow,
until my juices feed a savage sight
that runs along the lines, bright
as beasts' eyes. The rubble splays to dust:
city, book, bed, leaving my ear's lust
saying like Molly, yes, yes, yes O yes.

The Admiring Bog

I'm Nobody! Who are you?
Are you—Nobody—Too?
Then there's a pair of us!
Don't tell! they'd advertise—you know!

How dreary—to be—Somebody!
How public—like a Frog—
To tell one's name—the live-long June—
To an admiring Bog!

There is much joy in examining a poem, in scholarly analysis of its provenance, and fitting it into its historical slot. But this is an after-the-event joy, set in the original context of the poem itself. An even more fascinating adventure is consideration of that major basic event—the fact that the poem was written. Why? And for whom? And what effect, if any, has that whom upon the actual fabric of the poem?

Do the majority of good poets write primarily to express what they have a profound compulsion to express? Or is the basic compulsion that of communication and, if so, again with whom? With themselves, to discover who, as poets, they are? Or to call out, down as long a distance as is possible, to empathetic ears?

Is the creation of poetry to any degree actually dependent on the sense of communication, or are there truly many mute inglorious Miltons out there, who write because they must and will continue to do so, speaking as long as they have breath, to deaf ears?

And what of the treacheries of the Bog—how underfoot its

Adapted from a lecture delivered at Ohio University.

edges seem solid, until the foot gradually sinks into the quagmire of poetry biz—that necessary mélange of publications, editors, reviewers, grants, awards; that area in which the heartbeat is changed, not by recognition of the breathless felicity of a line but by the radiant or ominous first line of a review in the *New York Times*. There is no doubt whatsoever that when that last point is reached, the bog has become bog, indeed, and totally other in its composition and nature from the perilous, intimate, ferocious moment of poetic conception. And yet the descent is so dangerously gradual—and to some degree is also inevitable, since any body of poetic work canonized as distinguished will, with the inevitability of daybreak, pass through all these stages in reaching that ultimate objective, the reader.

Well, here is our poet, in his ritual attic, now often furnished in neo-NEA—writing his heart out. As a human being, he shares almost every vulnerability with the simplest or most complex forms of the animal life around him—hunger, fear, sex, death. But he is set apart by his dreadful opportunity—language. What is happening to him and around him and within him can be *told*. His predicament is unique. William Carlos Williams has said it boldly: "You have no other language for it but the poem." That is a big statement, but I believe it to be true. When strong emotional upheavals occur, even those with no raveling shred of poetic talent are driven to try poetry—witness the pathetic and boring reams spawned by events of no interest to anyone but the inarticulate author, someone ambushed by an adolescent crush or a joy huge in privacy but, exposed to the severity of language, a routine and banal experience; tributes to everything from a lost pet to a lost lover. The problem is, obviously, not with the subject matter but with the pitfall of the word. The editors of newspapers that never *publish* poetry (shall we call the majority?) reported that, immediately after the assassination of President Kennedy, they were deluged with masses of dreadful but passionately sincere poetry. These people were no more poets than they were kangaroos, but they had an obscure imperative: they understood that the language of prose, as they knew it, was incapable of expressing what it was that they needed to express, and they had a touching and basically valid instinct—that there must be another medium, and that that medium *must* be poetry.

Not that they would know a real poem if it bit them but that, down the ages, poetry has achieved a unique aura as the language that best expresses the inexpressible.

If we are forced to admit, by the helpless compulsion of non-poets who cannot accept prose as a medium for their distress or by Williams's words, that the genesis of true poetry is in a deep and unusual need, how does that come to terms with all the stages between conception and the admiring bog—that area of tangled voices and reactions and competitiveness and ephemerality? Perhaps the poet who examines these stages may tend to be more aware of how, inevitably, something that originally was valuable, in just the degree to which it was untouched by such considerations, imperceptibly ends immersed in them, and may be able to mark an invisible and necessarily flexible line, where the firm ground is traded for the fluctuating.

How much is recognition essential to the process of poetry? How many poets now widely recognized would have continued their work in the face of an apparent total rejection? We *are* able to say that that sort of rejection has a savage effect. When Keats, that touchstone, said in his youth and bitterness that his epitaph should be, "Here lies one whose name was writ in water," it was no epigram, it was more than the pain of a dying boy who feels that everything he has done will be accounted nothing. Keats felt always a kinship with the highest in poetry. He had not sufficient hubris to consider himself a young Shakespeare, but his idolatry of Shakespeare had, as its premise and ambition, that direction. He felt himself a true member of the company of the great—poets dead and gone—and he prized above everything that kinship. He had an intimate concept of the company of poets, the great world of poetry and its citizens, and to be part of the highest of that company was essential to him. When he was advised to return to his medical rounds, or mocked as a clown of poetry, it was bitter in exact proportion to his aspiration, and, indeed, to his belief in his own power. If that sort of rejection had continued—which seems inconceivable to us—would it have stamped out his fire? I doubt it. Would it have warped his emotions and soured his nature, as Frost's rejection well into his middle age did?

As we all know, when Frost sailed for England at the age of

forty, in the bog's sense, he was a total failure as a poet. Neither praised nor published, he suffered the corroding experience of knowing that he was a major poet, at the same moment that the bog's chorus passed him by, as completely as though he had not existed. Famous, lauded, a solon of the world of American poetry, he never, never regained the inner security he starved for and remained so insecure that the failure of a clerk in a New England motel or that of an elevator girl at the Library of Congress to recognize him could enrage—that is, frighten him.

No poet broods over the triumphs of Rod McKuen or of Harold Robbins—except, perhaps, financially. But to know the value of one's own work and to see specious poetry tripping about with a laurel wreath over one eye has been often a deeply damaging experience to the true poet.

One weighs that fact against the knowledge of a Gerard Manley Hopkins or an Emily Dickinson—contemporaries. Both were isolated from any audience. Hopkins, for a period, believed his poetry to be inimical to his vocation; Emily had fashioned herself a hermit's life to wear. Interestingly, both had poetic mentors interested in their work and stunningly unimaginative about the value of its unique characteristics. Yet Hopkins persisted in his alarming sprung rhythm and in his spiritual inscape and Emily in her poetic and staccato speech, as though there were no other way in which to write; and indeed, there was no other. And do we believe that Keats or Frost, finding no recognition, would have ceased as poet?

And now, what of the perils of the reverse? The widely recognized poet, early or late, has perils of his own that affect, and have always affected, poetry. Simple and obvious ones are the weight of expectations, the feedback in the inner ear, and the step too far into the bog.

Habit is a kind of kudzu, a smothering of intellectual sight. Every poet knows that few things are more important to his work than the ability truly to hear and see whether he is merely, in an altered or improved form, re-echoing work he has already done, the kind of work that is now associated with his name: the typical "resonance," to use a favored term, that has come to be associated with him, and which has become, to a degree, his trademark.

This danger, of the inner ear echo, merges into that of the

weight of expectations. In his marvelous little essay "Jazz," Matisse describes how Japanese artists of another era, once they had become famous, wearied by what was expected of them, established aesthetic identity by assuming a new name and starting from scratch, unhampered by the perceptions of pundits. Things get codified so quickly. Critics are sometimes as prone to a characteristic and inflexible response, as poets are endangered by their role. Classification is a scientific necessity, but it remains a literary danger. It can range from the empathetic and skillful discussion of the work to a dried and hubris-ridden set of "points," in which the debater surfaces in the guise of pundit. All of us have listened to him, in print or in person. Here, again, I fall back on my native language.

The Minor Poet

The minor poet sits at meat
with danger smoldering in his eye,
to left, to right, his dicta fly,
impaling those who blot or blotch:
should any dolt essay reply
his voice goes up another notch.

Attempts to qualify are doomed.
Who could object? Which would displease?
With fingers raised, in tones that freeze
he checks his points: 1, 2, 3, 4.
By salad time, the very cheese
is paler, for his scorn and lore.

Wit dies before his massy frown—
until, bethinking, from his files
he fetches forth a *mot,* and smiles!
And not a man or woman weeps,
though each one knows that we have miles
and miles to go before he sleeps.

There is one fascinating aspect of the cliché: it is an embalmed truth. That truth is there, indestructible, with truth's latent and savage force, but that truth has been smeared and smothered by usage in weary forms and must be recreated, and that is the poet's supreme challenge. It is like the relationship of a long-enduring love affair, in or out of marriage, in which the secret—and the necessity—is to keep uncovering the quick, the live marrow, which is constantly overlaid by the stealthy momentum of habit. True that there is nothing new under the sun, but all of the ancient things, the experiences basic to each human being, can be made new in the creative matrix. It is a formidable hazard, with the little alphabet and the unlimited knowledge—marvelous things arise, utterly created, utterly valid. But they must be the seed, the sperm of the poet's own—not his transformed playback from the throats of the bog. The thing is a perpetual menace.

We hear constantly of the fragmentation of our mental world, of our general assumptions: that widely held conclusions often no longer obtain. And nothing could be more true. We are splintered, indeed. And because the poet can count on no wide assumptions—or, worse, may be tempted by the ephemeral and chic assumptions of the season—there is a pressure to fill the vacuum with material that is response to a demand, rather than the explosion of a unique ability. Causes, circumstances, political or social, offer intellectual markets in which it is relatively easy for the poet to purchase passing attention. These causes and circumstances can trigger memorable work, but only if it is free of the supply-and-demand syndrome, if its roots go down to that layer of recognition, of acquiescence, in which the life of poetry pulses, from which, down the centuries, lines with undistinguished words, newly used, and common longings, alchemized to precious metal, come to us.

> Western wind, when wilt thou blow,
> The small rain down can rain?
> Christ, that my love were in my arms
> And I in my bed again!

The emotion is what any G. I. might and does feel; there is not an exotic word, but something has happened that prose never conceived and that the Bog never articulated.

Mr. James Kilpatrick, who is not notably fond of poetry, or of poets, has recently issued depressing statistics about the relative number of Americans to be found on a specific day in a major football stadium and the number destined voluntarily to read one poem in the course of a year. He feels poetry lacks a super-Bog, with its denizens all crying, "More, more, more!" And, indeed, when one's temper has died down, it is interesting to speculate about how it has happened that poetry has carried its aura of prestige, down the centuries; how it is still, secretly or overtly, regarded—even by those who would soon bed a porcupine as read a poem—as something special, something vaguely ethereal, something, they seem to imply, all too bright and good, or at least too irrelevant, for human nature's daily food.

So the poet is caught, to some degree, between these predicaments: the general incomprehension seems to throw him back into the competitive arena in which signs of appreciation and support, demand for what he feels compelled to do, exist. The Bog's voices, disguised as sirens' songs, pipe sweetly of publication, grants, of piney shelters with solitude, *and food cooked by someone else,* of reviews, and interviews, even, rarely enough, of sales. And how good these things are, in and of themselves. If the poet can detect clearly the seed of quid pro quo nestling there and plunge happily, but with ultimate caution, into the Bog's periphery, he is a cool hand.

The verdicts of the Bog tend to be cyclical. The general pattern being fame, obscurity, resurrection. Edith Wharton lamentably disappeared below the surface, as did Willa Cather. Now see their glorious surfacing!

Names swell in insidious ways: on the blurbs of jackets, in interviews, in lectures and readings, on committees and boards—all of them important, except possibly the blurb—but seasonal by-products, often taken for the product itself. André Malraux put it this way: "The first act, conscious or not, of all painters, is to change the function of objects." Some of the most perceptive critics have pointed out that great literature is not a ladder down that we descend in numerical order, gaining on some, leaving others behind. Instead, it is, above all, a simultaneous state occupied with poets dead and gone.

The one indestructible link in the succession is the similarity in caliber. This is why so much second-rate criticism misses the mark in its quest for the grand sequence. Sappho is no less contemporary than Dickinson, in the realm of poetry, George

Herbert than Gerard Manley Hopkins or Elizabeth Bishop. Sometimes we delude ourselves with the notion that contemporary subject matter makes for contemporary art. Contemporary art is living art; art ignores a date line. This is why so much poetry that has its impetus in cultural or political situations shrinks so rapidly with age. Situations constantly alter themselves, and, their date line removed, the work shrinks.

It would be heartening to think that the Bog has no terrors for those whose work has both quality and an admiring audience. But Leonard Woolf would never allow Virginia to see a review of her work that he had not previously vetted. May Sarton was made ill, and canceled a trip to Japan, after an unfavorable review of her poetry appeared in the *New Yorker,* and letters and biographies are full of the record of wounds and damage from the writing of critics of no special stature. The poet is perhaps even more vulnerable to hostility instead of admiration than other artists, because his offering is a peculiarly vulnerable part of himself, even though his poetry is not the kind labeled as confessional. After all, notes and pigment provide some sort of screen for their users, albeit a fragile one. But words have a dictionary meaning, though they are never identical to the poet's use, and a sort of awful responsibility-to-definition exists, which can put the poet on the defensive unless he is a very cool customer indeed.

Then there is the tricky desire to please—to lure that cobra out of its basket—to walk that tightrope, to demonstrate that you are a professional, and that your work is *relevant,* that sacred word . . .

When I was Poetry Consultant to the Library of Congress, a very nice gentleman from the Goddard Space Center came to the Library to see me and complained most bitterly that poets hated the space program. I tried to tell him that I honestly didn't think that was true, that many of them simply grudged funds denied to things they felt were more urgently needed. But he remained disheartened and asked me if I and my husband would come to the center and watch a space trip charted. We went, and very impressive indeed it was—the great darkened room, the lights so distant and mysterious that were traveling across that immense blackness.

A week later our friend returned to the poetry office. He wanted to know, with a terribly seductive eagerness, if I had written a poem. I had not. And I must admit that seldom have I felt a guiltier sense of not measuring up, of having refused to practice my professed art. Those two interviews have been exemplary for me in the whole matter of the seductiveness of the Bog and the poet's dogged knowledge that, unlike the leader of a band, he cannot respond with a request number, however complimentary and appealing the plea. I would have *loved* to have illuminated the mysteries, the ironies, the stupendous beauties of space travel. But what passes for my muse had not stirred a hair, and, had I come with a response, it would have been, as the hospitals succinctly put it, DOA.

If request-minus-desire is fatal to the poet, one has only to contrast the ghastly effusions of most of the early poets laureate of England with an exquisite contemporary epithet-lamium in which skill, desire, and occasion marry, to see that, even in this area, generalization is fragile.

In the case of the Bog, as in most things, it is a matter of nuances—almost imperceptibly, the worthy shallows of much-to-be-desired praise from sound critics, and honorable awards, of editorial tastes, good or bad reviews, can lead on and on to the spot at which the poem sinks into the morass of competition, logrolling, and the pursuit of the chic.

The true depth finder is the standard of the best poetry that has been written. Nothing else so quickly identifies the second-rate and the derivative.

To say that criticism has only negative value is to say that it remains crucially important. Though no line of criticism ever written has been a substitute for that creative energy that is the poem's seedbed, a fine critic accomplishes the next most important thing: he can diagnose the self-inflicted ills of the poet.

While I was with the Library of Congress, we held a national symposium on courses in creative writing. Good or bad in their ultimate results? Helpful or destructive in creative development? We called on the heads of four famous departments—Wallace Stegner of California, John Ciardi of Breadloaf, Paul Engle of Iowa, and Elliott Coleman of the Johns Hopkins Writing Seminars. Each head produced for us his proudest product, who then also gave a talk. It was noisy and great and lavishly attended. At the end, when the dust settled, after differing viewpoints, teaching theories, personalities and theories, amazingly a more or less unified conclusion did emerge—that it was doubtful if any course could accomplish more than its supremely important task, negative but vital: the identification of the soft spot, the fatal tendency to self-destruction. Surely writers so alerted, so prevented from self-defeat, are better writers and should be grateful—and hope for nothing more esoteric or miraculous. But the result is also pitiless. True poetry is arbitrary and unpurchasable. If we ever forget that and think that it can be custom tailored, acquired, or taught or learned, we are deluded.

I believe that the greatest claims for poetry are not extravagant. What would be ludicrous hubris when applied to the poet can be justified as applied to poetry itself. That sense of the magic—the basically undefinable magic—that is the core of poetry is like nothing else in language. It is what Frost meant when he said of translation that the untranslated element was the poem. The best poetry, when we meet it, imposes a deep acquiescence, a profound affirmation. It can never be imitated, and it can never be totally analyzed.

I can think of no subject matter too slight or too lowly for the poet's use—Shapiro has his housefly, Donne his flea, Blake his worm. The poetry will take care of the significance. At a time in which disillusionment and lively cynicism are hard to resist, it may seem anachronistic to speak and think in terms of greatness. We are shy in the face of superlatives—and rightly. But poetry itself, that seed, that element, is magic and eternal. And though everything around us, from the political speech to the advertisement, tends to make us shrink from giant claims, we can make them solidly for the core of poetry.

When one considers the twenty-six little letters of the alphabet and the recurrence and simplicity of poetry's major themes—fear, loss, love, death—there is a breath-taking glimpse of the creative force of that element that is poetry, permanent, tough, disconnected from the encroachments of the Bog that is its neighbor.

The sense of kinship with poets, dead and gone, is for some

one of the sustaining aspects of poetry. Regardless of the poet's place in the pantheon, for him the poets down the ages are presences often more real than those of the hat-check girl a foot away or the fellow guest into whose ear he shouts at a cocktail party. To excuse myself by Williams's dictum, I found that in this lecture what I most wanted to express was expressed by a poem of mine:

The Chinese Insomniacs

It is good to know
the Chinese insomniacs.
How, in 495 A.D.,
in 500 B.C.,
the moon shining, and the pine-
trees shining back
at it, a poet had to walk
to the window.

It is companionable
to remember my fellow
who was unable to sleep
because of a sorrow, or not;
who had to watch
for the wind
to stir night flowers in the garden
instead of making the deep journey.

They live nine hun-
dred years apart,
and turn, and turn, restless.
She says her sleeve is wet
with tears; he says something difficult
to forget, like
music counts the heartbeat.

A date is only a mark
on paper—it has little to do
with what is long.
It is good to have their company
tonight: a lady, awake
until birdsong;
a gentleman who made
poems later out of frag-
ments of the dark.

II
Reviews and Criticism

Frost, Cummings, Williams
Legacy of Three Poets

When the exhibit "The Image of Man" toured the museums of the country, sooner or later, in each city, there was a note of dismay, if not of protest: is *this* how the artist sees man, sees life in his own day? Often tragic and horrifying, always sobering, this show was in fact one more sign that the vast majority of twentieth-century artists—whether painters, novelists, sculptors, playwrights, or poets—have found the face of contemporary life a Medusa visage. The point needs no laboring. Anyone through whose hands any part of the torrent of poetry pours knows that most of the best of it deals with frustration, helpless pain, betrayed integrity, and a desolate and piercing sense of dislocation.

In the past twelve months three prominent American poets died: Robert Frost, E. E. Cummings, and William Carlos Williams. All were old—between seventy and ninety—and, in our general conception, old age is a period alien, if not fatal, to poetry. The Shelley-Keats image, the youthful figure of the runner fame never outran, lingers, and Yeats—that poet who flowered most fully when he was so close to death—was aware, in *Sailing to Byzantium,* of the conventionality of "cooling poet and burning poem."

Whether there is that in contemporary living that is auspicious for the poetry of maturity might be worth wondering about. It is possible that a poetry of which the core is endurance had to be written by poets who had passed the age that finds endurance

---

From *Commonweal,* 10 May 1963.

impossible or ignoble. In any event, the three poets who died in the past year continued in their later lives to deepen and extend their own work, and this work gives to the reader who asks himself in what its core consists the opportunity to examine poetry that reached its highest level when the men who produced it were able to speak from great reserves of experience.

In considering these American poets, more than midway through the twentieth century and in relation to the atmosphere they breathed in their country and their age, one fact emerges: these three were profoundly different one from another in background, in temperament, in technique. But in a curious way they are alike. They are alike in that their verdict, the quintessence of the vision of life that their work represents, differs from the general tone of the artist today. None of the three ever overlooks, denies, or minimizes the poison or pitfall. None of them has an iota of easy optimism, and none of them covers any grim shape with a coat of gilt. Whatever sense of ultimate order, meaning, or hope their work posits rises like a spring from below the roots of factual knowledge. It never comes, superficially, from above these roots. For each of the three a faith is the condition of his work.

These poets do not deny any of the imputations of those who write in a state of mind close to despair. They are no more pleased by the accomplishments of authority or the circumstances of survival than are Beckett or Camus or Orwell. They acknowledge the details of an image they reject, but they do more than this. They pass from these things, which they acknowledge in the very bone and structure of their work, to something living and unquenchable that absorbs all that deadly knowledge and in the end uses it to quicken a final yet tentative vision.

That vision, in each of the poets, has a serenity, a sense of life and richness that denies the facts only by translating them. This is not "significant" as a "trend." It does not argue a shift toward optimism on the part of the artist. It means simply itself, that at a moment when many people feel stranded between the Kafkaesque inferno of chaos—a chaos all the more sinister for being suspected of having immutable and mysterious laws—and the waxworks of positive thinking, three of America's most independent poets have ended by leaving at the core of their poetry a belief in a hopeful design.

One of the tragedies of modern language is that certain words captured and gutted by the enemy have remained in captivity, tottering about as hideous clichés. Poets have, reasonably enough, become convinced that words such as *love* and *beauty* now exist as embarrassing and faintly obscene travesties. It is only a step from this conviction to outlawing from honest work not only the words but their implications. Each of these poets has resolved that dilemma.

Robert Frost is a poet who has suffered spectacularly from a specious approachability. People who were unwilling to read difficult poetry, or incapable of reading it, conceived, with a sublime ignorance, that they were able to read Frost. Consequently, the fatuous seeker after poetically respectable clichés has often sustained an image of him as an apple-cheeked, twinkle-eyed, cracker-barrel bard, full of wholesome no-nonsense. In their efforts to destroy this lampoon, Frost's critics were driven to point out, truthfully, the profoundly somber nature of his outlook, the strain of implacable loneliness and darkness that runs through the core of his poetry. The final weight of Frost's conviction of, and acquiescence in, an order governing visible chaos rests in large part just on this sense of loneliness and darkness.

The quintessence of Frost's vision of nature has under its measured serenity a shiver of the power of darkness that it has surmounted and controlled. Frost loves the verb *to scare.* It has a misleading sound of the childish, almost of the cute. But in the context of fear, of evil, it is the doll, the child, which can be most frightening. Frost uses *scare* as the witch of Coös mislays the skeleton's knuckle bone among the buttons in her sewing bag. From very early poems to "The Draft Horse"—that finest poem of Frost's last collection—this sense of fear, a fear in which silence, night, the soul of darkness, has invaded the physical, is omnipresent.

> They learned to rattle the lock and key
> To give whatever might chance to be

Warning and time to be off in flight:
And preferring the out- to the in-door night
They learned to leave the house-door wide
Until they had lit the lamp inside.

We do not need the later nightmare adventure of "The Draft Horse" to teach us that this is not fear of a tramp, a murderer, or of a puppet of social evil but of a faceless ancient foe; the dry rattle of a shutter, a phone ringing in an empty room, the malevolence of a windy autumn night—something powerful and evil, interrupted. "Out on the porch's sagging floor / Leaves got up in a coil and hissed, / Blindly struck at my knee and missed." These actions, this weather, correspond to that "inner weather" of the poet, who can scare himself with his "own desert places."

In "The Draft Horse" the dark knife that strikes, killing the horse and leaving the protagonist and his companion to go "with a lantern that wouldn't burn / Through a pitch-dark, limitless grove," smacks clearly of hate. And hate is indeed considered and rejected. What is tentatively accepted is that this is not a vicious device to trap and lose the victims in limitless pitch-darkness. This is a faith in design (nothing more than design) that is neither naive, optimistic, nor specific.

Frost's pleasure in "ulteriority" is nowhere more evident than in his use of the homespun accent; nothing baffles faster. A public that for seventy-five years conceived *Huckleberry Finn* as a rollicking children's book and the source of summer posters is not likely to find the "ingredients of a witch's broth" or the details of an Ingmar Bergman forest at dusk in a child's jingle such as "We dance around in a ring and suppose, / But the secret sits in the middle and knows."

The sense of serenity that is ultimately found to be the basis of Frost's work does not pretend to take a new view of the materials for hope. Their aspect is hopeless; it is from the hopelessness itself that the poet gathers hope, from the nature of its secret that he gathers his fruit, rooted below the level of possibility's contradiction: "What tree may not the fig be gathered from? / The grape may not be gathered from the birch? / It's all you know the grape, or know the birch."

There is a timeless quality in Frost's work that irrationally argues that he was born mature; one watches the poetry of William Carlos Williams achieve maturity. But if E. E. Cummings ever had maturity thrust upon him, he repulsed it cleanly. In his bumpy introduction to the *Collected Poems* (which begins with what must surely be the coyest introduction to open any book, "The poems to come are for you and for me and are not for mostpeople . . ."). Cummings says, "Take the matter of being born. What does being born mean to mostpeople? Catastrophe unmitigated . . . Social revolution. The cultured aristocrat yanked out of his hyper-exclusive ultravoluptuous superpallazzo, and dumped into an incredibly vulgar detention camp, swarming with every conceivable species of undesirable organism." And this attitude of hostile derision toward the denigration of life never alters in the long, uneven history of Cummings's work. The derision is uneven, too. Much of its springs from Cummings's deliberately willed immaturity, from his determination to ignore things he does not wish to acknowledge.

Time has been ruthless to much of his bitterness and most of his vituperation. Even the figures in good poems have had the ground snatched from under them. Olaf and Miss Gay only survive at all because of an archetypal truth that sustains them, regardless of factual circumstances surrounding female college students and conscientious objectors. But the obverse of the derision toward life haters was Cummings's own completely spontaneous and indestructible confidence in the value of being alive.

To Cummings's eyes, knaves and fools surround him. He is persecuted by systems, pressures, rigidities. But all his protests, valid and puerile alike, are secondary to his true impetus. He is, at bottom, only interested in these things as obstacles. Never do they constitute for him, as for many a heartsick artist, all that seems left in a shrunken life. Through the embarrassing misses, the clear jazzy hits, the jejune absurdities, runs the flood of true passion. It may express itself in Cole Porter wisdom: "there is a lady whose name is afterwards. / she is sitting beside young death, is slender / likes flowers." It is present in the feel of things ostensibly joyless: "Satanic and blasé / a black goat lookingly wanders"; or "the queer monkey, with a little oldish doll-like face and hairy arms like an ogre and rubbercolored hands and feet filled with quick fingers and a remarkable tail which is allbyitselfalive." It is overt in every "brittle marvelous breathing thing."

"Rain is no respecter of persons / the snow doesn't give a soft white / damn Whom it touches." But below this there is a level of far greater intensity. As Frost is conscious of a hostile intent somewhere, which is resolved in the consciousness of design, so Cummings feels, directly, a presence of benignancy—"deeply completely conscious of the rain or rather / Somebody who uses roofs and streets skillfully to make a possible beautiful sound."

In proportion as he succeeds as a lyric poet, it is happily difficult to pin Cummings down, and at his absolute best he is, magnificently, a lyric poet. The joy, the sense of receiving without ever possessing, which is his greatest characteristic, is conveyed in a cadence, a tone or a vowel, or by the hesitations within a line. And it is in this way, far more than in what he specifies, that Cummings functions in his role as believing man. Yet he is specific, in his manner:

   (make
strangely) known (establish
new) come, what
Being! open us open
our
selves, create
(suddenly announce: hurl
blind full steep love)

Cummings's last, and even his best, poems are still freely mingled with the old embarrassing spit-in-your-eye cuteness, self-righteous clamor, and look-ma-no-hands maneuvers. But, conversely, beginning very early and with total consistency, there is one quality that runs through everything, and it does steady and fortify itself.

There can seldom have been a poet who devoted more of his time reviling systems, people, methods of thought, and groups. It is possible to discover under the wildly assorted objects of his wrath a common principle: death-in-life. It is deadness and its corruption of life, its injury to life, against which Cummings launched both his spitballs and his thunderbolts. Religiosity, conformity, nationalism, the police mind, the possessive, are by him all lumped into one characteristic. They are hostile to life, to the principle of growth, of spring, of creation. They are important to him not of themselves but because of their obdurate weight thrown against life's motions. "Miracles are to come. With you I leave a remembrance of miracles; they are by somebody who can love and who shall be continuously reborn, a human being; somebody who said to those near him when his fingers would not hold a brush, 'tie it into my hand.' "

Besides the perfecting of a form and approach more flexible than Frost's, more sustained than Cummings, the poetry of William Carlos Williams fuses two forces often viewed as hostile: the leap of joy and the sense of moral structure. In common with Frost and Cummings, Williams as a poet is never one of the self-deprecators—the poets who have a final shattering sense of their own unimportance, of their own voices as faintly ludicrous, piping in the general chaos. He makes for the role of poet large and ancient claims:

> I have eyes
> that are made to see and if
> they see ruin for myself
> and all that I hold
> dear, they see
> also
> through the eyes
> and through the lips
> and tongue the power
> to free myself and speak of it.

It is possible that no other American poet—and Williams was profoundly and almost ostentatiously American—has so delicately balanced the point of chaos and its domination. His postulated victory is made from a thousand failures, blunders, absurdities, and cruelties. His ultimate conviction of the nature of commitment, and of its relation to love and to joy, is reached by receiving and dominating all assaults.

Karl Shapiro once asked: "What has become of the love poem?" Answer: William Carlos Williams has written it. "Asphodel, That Greeny Flower" is a love poem as fine as any written in English in the last fifty years. From it Williams's form emerges, complex in simplicity, strong, and delicately balanced. And from it, too, emerge the shapes of continuity and love, of continuity in love, the odor of the asphodel:

> It is a curious odor,
> a moral odor,
> that brings me
> near to you.

The poem is alive with discovery. Williams refuses formulas—he has spoken hotly of the poets who are "pimps of tradition." Nor can he be accused of ingenuousness in his warmth or in his faith in commitment. In whatever sense *Paterson* may fail, certainly it does not fail from lack of the sense of reality. As poet, as physician, Williams is an unbemused observer:

> Faces all knotted up like burls on oaks
> Grasping, fox-spouted, thick-lipped,
> Sagging breasts and protruding stomachs,
> Rasping voices, filthy habits with the hands.

What Williams did in life and what he did not do have enormously influenced the poems. The physician is implicit in the peculiarly trained lucidity with which he observes physical, emotional, and mental states, and it is this in turn that makes so impressive his sense of a whole, which is more than the sum of physique, nervous system, and emotions. What he did not do was affiliate himself with literary cliques, fronts, competitiveness, academic rivalries. He is the least inky of poets.

It is interesting that, while (due as much to the necessities of their profession as to their own taste) a heavy plurality of all poets today are associated with some academic institution, Williams, Frost, and Cummings are all exceptions to this rule. Each was by temperament unsuited to academic life, and each was notably "unliterary" in his flavor. Though in each the fruit was quite different, the roots were all strongly in the idiom of daily speech, and each ran counter to certain poetic assumptions common to the hour in which his poetry began to assume its distinctive form.

As his final poems perfect the order toward which his work had been struggling—the strong, accurate, characteristic shape that was imposed by Williams on the turbulent mass of his material—so they speak of another order, an order that imposed itself on the chaos of phenomena:

> I have learned much in my life
> from books
> and out of them
> about love.
> Death
> it is not the end of it

Poet of the Particular

Just because today's poet is so separated from the general reader, his success is less vulnerable and more dangerous. Once launched on the full current of a major success, his maneuvers reach the general public via the voice of the critic and of the yea-sayers who have become the critic's chorus. Inertia is as powerful a force in poetry as in any other form of motion.

People are frightened, and guilty, and hungry for illumination, and, if a poet tells them what to think about fright and guilt and the hope of escape from confusion, they are grateful—they are grateful even if it is someone else who tells them that the poet is telling them. This produces a situation ripe for the pseudo-poetry of commentary, kept afloat by its subject matter; the sea is dotted with such craft. Such pseudo-poetry is, above all, characterized by the sense of smartness; the wail for current woes terminates on a note of self-satisfaction, a fashionable mourning less interested in communicating distress than in demonstrating its own right-thinkingness; poetry ending not with a pang but a simper.

Side by side with the topical *arrivistes,* there spring up poets whose contribution to the comprehension of their own age is no less real and penetrating for being oblique. Poets such as Theodore Roethke, whose poems about stones and greenhouses and birds relate to everything in human consciousness, do not need to discuss war or hypocrisy in order to illuminate them. Then there are the few poets—the very few—whose natural idiom is that of history, or the individual human event; who do not have to pervert, or even divert, their poetry from its natural

From *Commonweal,* 4 December 1964.

functioning, when they write poems set deeply, and overtly, in consideration of a caste or a city or an era. Robert Lowell is an outstanding example of this last sort of poet. Often he has had a bad press for silly reasons; often he has had fantastic praise for reasons scarcely less silly. One critic has said that in the presence of his poetry we must be grateful and not inquire; he has been praised for errors and lapses; at the moment it would appear that he can scarcely do wrong.

It is Lowell himself who has said, "In poetry, tone is everything." He is fortunate in his tone. It fluctuates in strength: infrequently, it bogs down; more often, it pitches into a buzz of violence. But its characteristic is a scorching sincerity. Sincerity at this pitch being too painful to be sustained without break, break this occasionally does, into a blatant, and often unsuccessful, showmanship. But its quality and its power to shake are irresistible.

From Lowell's emergence, in the days of *Lord Weary's Castle* to *For the Union Dead,* his tone is that of a Jeremiah, reluctantly versed in Freud. The overtones are biblical; the worldly message is of woe. "Flies, flies are in the plane trees, on the streets." He is acutely aware of the ambivalence of the sense of guilt and of its capacity for resentment.

> Father, forgive me
> my injuries,
> as I forgive
> those I
> have injured!

The theme of "suffering without purgation" has a dozen variations. The Lowell image of wild tearless spiders crying together carries vibrations straight from Jonathan Edwards, the subject of one of Lowell's best poems, and he ejaculates: "Pity the monsters! Pity the monsters! . . . My heart bleeds black blood for the monsters." The decay of time without moral achievement haunts Lowell. His poetry's needle swings from "all's possible, all's unpredictable" to the sorrowful "Washington in July": "The elect, the elected . . . they come here bright as dimes and die disheveled and soft."

Death is a presence never far from any Lowell poem. In *Poems 1938–1949* twenty-three out of forty-two poems deal, in some degree, specifically with death. Violence, guilt, disloyalty, in history and in the individual, are all set, for proportion, before the face of death. As a presence, as a question, it is all-implicit; into it the simplest images blandly crash. If the poet glances out of his window:

> Three stories down below,
> A choreman tends our coffin's length of soil,
> and seven horizontal tulips blow.

As in "Death from Cancer" and "In Memory of Arthur Winslow," many of Lowell's finest poems are poems to the dead. In this poetry—not happily but hauntingly religious in accent—question after question is tacitly put to the unanswering figure.

Given this quality of rooted, perpetual examination, Lowell's approach is through a fusion of compassion and violence. The unaffected violence gives his work much of its nervous system; a high proportion of the poetry functions by violent perceptions and reactions. At no time has Lowell's poetry foreseen less than violence: "There were shod hoofs beneath the horseplay." In prose he remarks, simply, "one had the feeling that our lives were being lived in the brutal, fashionable expectancy of the stadium." But if the world of mores and associations is based on violence, the violence becomes only more powerful and mysterious in less mundane matters. At Christmas: "Tonight, my child, the foot-loose hallows stalk us down in the blind alleys of our rooms"; and, after a death, one line: "Two angels fought with bill-hooks for his soul."

It is important that this violence is never the quasi-bogus, contra-conventional reflex of the more energetic Beat poets. Lowell is not bent on shattering conventions, literary or otherwise; he is too inattentive toward familiar unimportant objects. He is confronting a chaos in which are formed, with blinding precision, ephemeral patterns, conceivably fractions of a larger and invisible pattern. He crystallizes the pattern, often with full use of his enormous skill, and always with the knowledge of its ephemeral nature, against the dark background he habitually

acknowledges. His compassion, curiously the more compelling for seeming itself so painfully and forcibly compelled, is like a hot, involuntary outburst of grief. The sense of suffering, detailed and relentless, communicates itself in an arc so wide as to be poetically inescapable. The turtles of "The Neo-Classical Urn" are germane to the lobster of Samuel Beckett's "Dante and the Lobster," in a confounding of proportion and scale.

Emerging from its primary considerations, Lowell's poetry comes full upon two of its major problems—which are, perhaps, ultimately one. He has an affinity for history. From the time when, as a child, he coveted the lead soldier replicas of Kleber, Marshal Ney, Murat, and the king of Naples to "For the Union Dead," he has found his field in history, or in that special sort of literary history afforded by the work of other writers. This approach, which, in the hands of the mildly talented, leads straight to the occasional poem and the attempt to graft weak stock on strong, in the hands of a poet of Lowell's ability is like the time proffered by Frost's illuminated clock against the sky—neither wrong nor right. It is merely hazardous. Lowell has used the work of other men and the stories of flexible history to a degree unknown in the work of any other outstanding contemporary poet: translations that are not translations but poems "after" the work of another writer, incidents, public and private, embroidered, altered, transubstantiated; very few of his poems escape, or intend to escape, the previous enunciation of someone else.

Oddly enough, this never seems to affect Lowell's originality. What it does affect is the quality of his poetry. Unless the incident, the poem, the man, is taken up purely into the whirlwind of Lowell's creativity, the resulting work is injured. It is as though from the hat into which the conjuror has caused the dove to disappear, fell a feather, a coral claw—a result at once macabre and disappointing. And it is at this point and on encountering these poems that one remembers longingly the aliases of the Japanese artists—those sequential names, fragrant with anonymity. For now and then one feels that Lowell is being pushed into the thing he least desires: a posture. The implacable shove of his success seems to require, more and more, that he be the one to "Say It," "It" being whatever contemporary comment is most required at the moment. He has the power, and he has, often, the magic, for transubstantiation. He needs every shred of it. Too often there is the feeling that he has seized, roughly, material that has set off for him the poetic process and then presented it to his own gaze and that of others as his poem, when it is only the oyster's irritation. He writes some bad poems; worse, he ruins some terribly good ones.

The August issue of *Show* published the text of *Benito Cereno,* one of two verse plays by Lowell currently running in New York under the title "Old Glory." *Benito Cereno* derives, very closely, from Herman Melville's formidable story of masks and their violation of relationships, which derives, in turn, from *A Narrative of Voyages and Travels in the Northern and Southern Hemispheres: Comprising Three Voyages Round the World; Together with a Voyage of Survey and Discovery, in the Pacific Ocean and Oriental Islands,* by Amasa Delano (Boston, 1817). Melville's story is no less magnificent for his having taken this at least reasonably factual material and turned it to his own somber, ornate, and terrifying uses; in Melville's story, Lowell has found precisely the violent, ambiguous, and bizarre stuff to nourish his poetic imagination. What could be more congenial to Lowell's muse than the language and tone of Melville's perception? "The San Dominick had been battledored about by contrary winds, inveigled by currents or grown weedy in calms"; or "As intense heat and cold, though unlike, produce like sensations, so innocence and guilt, when through casual association with mental pain, stamping any visible impress, use one seal—a hacked one."

The poem, considered here primarily as poem, that Lowell has produced from this echo of an echo of an adventure has an ambience of terror and beauty. It has been made all his own, and he has replaced Melville's stunning artifice of fluctuating tensions, of a world at once sealed, remote, and nightmarishly here and real, by his own sharper and less leisurely sense of doom, and Melville's final laconic irony by a more limited and direct thrust. But there hovers over the work a sense of obligation, of delivering the goods, of coming through. It is not sufficient to corrupt the poem, only enough to cause a faint nostalgic wonder about what Lowell might have done with a less demanding target—or with no target at all.

For the Union Dead is Lowell's least uneven book. It is strong

on the characteristics that give his poetry its true stature, a ferocious humility, immediate vitality, and a pervasive and extraordinary generosity of spirit. It is filled with lines that palpitate with differing sorts of energy:

> The muskrat that took a slice of your thumb still huddles,
> a mop of hair and a heart-beat on the porch—
>
> there's the tin waste-basket where it learned to wait
> for us playing dead, the slats it mashed in terror,
> its spoor of cornflakes, and the packing crate
> it furiously slashed to matchwood to escape.

Lines of re-creation, in a kind of fiery nostalgia:

> Everything's changed for the best—
> how quivering and fierce we were,
> there snowbound together,
> simmering like wasps
> in our tent of books!

Lines of intimacy and tension between the detail and the whole:

> my life's fever is soaking in night sweat—
> one life, one writing! But the downward glide
> and bias of existing wrings us dry—
> always inside me is the child who died,
> always inside me is his will to die—
> one universe, one body . . . in this urn
> the animal night sweats of the spirit burn.

Lowell is uncannily aware of the desert spots in what we think of as our conscious life; of the strange blank cells that Valéry reminds himself are not taken into account: "my absences, my deep, long, insensible variations. I forget that I possess in my own life a thousand models of death, of daily nothingness, an astonishing quantity of lacunae, of things suspended, of intervals unknowing and unknown." Lowell's humor is largely used to pin down proportion; he has an almost horrified distrust of the morally inaccurate: "the serpent's flawed, euphoric hiss." In this book there is less of the muddy, of the poetically unresolved,

than in *Life Studies,* for example. There is less of the vision so private, left so surrounded by dark that it dazzles and blinds instead of illuminating. There is less of the sense of using poetry as a personal catharsis.

The skill of the poetry has continued to increase; one of Lowell's functional triumphs is his ability to drive a poetic device to what should be the point of exhaustion and have it seem the poem's spontaneous pulse. In the lightest lines a sardonic affability will be under iron discipline. He does sometimes still allow his knowledge that the amazing hint is often the poem's backbone to dictate, even beyond the discovery that in a given instance it is a mistake—and, when this happens, a poem that has taken a wrong direction is allowed to follow it to a conclusion that is striking but self-destructive as well.

It is difficult to write of Lowell's poetry without using injured words: *love, honor, salvation.* Almost no poem fails to relate to one of these, seen, down the perspectives of history, finally in contemporary terms. Human inability to love frightens him: "When we try to kiss / Our eyes are slits and cringing, and we hiss."

In the book's title poem—its last and best—a circle is closed. As a child, Lowell had watched the circular, silent, valueless world of the fish tank:

> Once my nose crawled like a snail on the glass;
> my hand tingled
> to burst the bubbles
> drifting from the noses of the cowed, compliant fish.

After life, sacrifice, and death, Colonel Shaw and his Negro infantry are a bronze monument, shaken by the gouging, encroaching, grunting, yellow dinosaurs of the steam shovels.

> He is out of bounds now. He rejoices in man's lovely
> peculiar power to choose life and die—
> when he leads his black soldiers to death,
> he cannot bend his back.
>
> On a thousand small town New England greens,
> the old white churches hold their air

of sparse sincere rebellion; frayed flags
quilt the graveyards of the Grand Army of the Republic.

"The Ditch is nearer," says Lowell. "Space is nearer." And the immediate view is terribly similar to the fish tank world. The hand that itched to break the fishes' bubbles has not done so. Where is that Colonel Shaw—trapped too? The "Aquarium" is gone from sight, for we are in it now.

Colonel Shaw
is riding on his bubble,
he waits
for the blessèd break.

The Aquarium is gone. Everywhere
giant finned cars nose forward like fish;
a savage servility
slides by on grease.

It is so fine a poem that one can only pray that Lowell will not be coerced by its brilliance into imitating it; he is being cast in a role, and it takes the most confident ability to wait, to escape that kind of casting. If Lowell is not yet consistently nearly so good as his most unrestrained admirers assert, he is so truly good that he cannot become a sort of Mr. Twentieth Century by vote of his critics and peers. He has, certainly, gifts peculiarly suitable to this classification, but they are viable just because their roots go down to ancient and common sources. If he can escape Poetry Business, if he can continue his poetry's wayward development, we are going to be fortunate. Translations, plays, libretti—all are likely enough vehicles for the flexible energy of his poetry. But not necessary ones.

The horrid injunction "Think Big" continues to blink on and off in neon lights over the heads of poets. Lowell's poem "Hawthorne" ends, "Hawthorne, thinking on the true / and insignificant." What a pure and furious antidote to Think Big; with that taken to heart, no alias would seem necessary as safeguard for a poet's liberty. To think that all those who have succeeded, as they look back on the difficulties of their start in life, are able to exclaim with conviction, "Those were the good days!"

For most of them success has meant a prison, and the artist must never be a prisoner. Prisoner? An artist must never be a prisoner even of himself, a prisoner of style, a prisoner of reputation, a prisoner of good fortune. Did not Matisse, like the Goncourt brothers, tell us that Japanese artists of the great period changed their names several times in their lifetimes? This pleases me: they wanted to safeguard their liberties.

History as Death

With Robert Lowell the historical sense is a passion, almost an obsession. It is never escaped. The most intimate incident, the most obscure observation, is left as part of the sweep of history. This is a history highly subjective, watched through preoccupations and expressed by ambiguities and a shock technique of the bizarre and the grotesque.

Mr. Lowell shakes history loose from its formal proportions to see where it carries us. In his work his life appears as the history of a mitigated disaster, his history as the disaster of human life. If he never snaps off the view with the almost smug cynicism of the despairing, it is only because he respects the possibilities of the unexpected.

Inevitably, this equating of his poetry with history conditions everything in his work. Ionesco has described the artist as a member of the "extra-historical community," quoting as his moment a timeless one in which "philosopher and shoemaker, 'master' and 'slave,' priest and layman are reconciled and indistinguishable." Dylan Thomas and Theodore Roethke function within this moment; Mr. Lowell never does.

What gives his poetry its stature—and, at all times, this it has—is the phenomenon of the sense of history expressed in a jagged series of shocks of varying, and often great, intensity and of an absolute sincerity. This is more than his technique; it is itself his means of communication.

Often it fails, the rational too oblique, the surreal too subordinated to reason, so that both misfire, and the poem stutters and

---

A review of *Notebook 1967–1968* by Robert Lowell, from *Baltimore Sun*, 15 June 1969.

falls in glittering fragments. The inclusion is too catholic; often it is as though Mr. Lowell felt that exclusion was in some way cowardly or treacherous: if the poem is mutilated, or involuntarily incoherent, it is an honorable casualty; it must be kept.

In the "Notebook" the facet of history that most concerns Mr. Lowell is death. It is perhaps another name for history: what was. His personal death, its prevision, its stages, dominate the tone. The book is forehaunted by that day when "his pinch of dust lies on the eternal dust-tray, lies on call forever, never called." There is never enough time. Only eternity would be enough.

The pace is tremendous. Each poem crashes open, noisily or silently spilling its contents. Often poems on historical characters open on a racing angle, which scarcely gives the poet time to strike his target before the final word lies there.

What, he demands, is inside? What is this thing, person, event, made of? What will it have said in history? Doctors as raccoons, Abelard as a fish, Mary McCarthy as a self-envisioned Jeanne d'Arc, politicians as ballerinas, God as H_2O.

Mr. Lowell says that these 150 pages of nonsonnet, fourteen-line sections, are one poem; not a chronicle, not a diary; a notebook. Hence, arbitrary, nonsequential, answering only to a private sense of proportion. If you want to read only the best of Mr. Lowell, a lot of these poems must be left out. If you are interested primarily in an encounter with the Lowell oeuvre, the mind and heart of Lowell as poet-historian, not one can be omitted.

Some of the (many) poems about identified people are among the least satisfactory: one slanting impression, like a nose reflected in a silver teaspoon, carrying off the poem in a burst of misproportion. Others (e.g., those on Ford Maddox Ford, Che Guevara, Robert Kennedy, Harpo Marx) are marvelously good and moving.

With each of Mr. Lowell's books the sense grows that there is a book coming in which everything—absolutely everything—necessary to his poetry will be seined, will be there carrying the full weight of his look at life, with the shards, flukes, prophylactic incantations, vanished, having served their turn.

In 1969 guilt is our thing; what gout was to the aging nobles of British fiction guilt is to us: suitable, painful, and prestigious.

But these poems wear their guilt with a difference. It is omnipresent, but it is large, even noble. It is not the paranoiac guilt-for-kicks, or even vanity in disguise. It is the ancient and true melancholy; it has its roots and is trying to grow toward some sort of purgation.

It would be much too easy, as well as simplistic, to say that Mr. Lowell's poetry more and more presses on the pain of a religious necessity. But it is certainly true that whatever trust he has in life or happiness is located in a source out of time; in history he understands evil best.

In the end, what a relief to read a large poetry. The flaws are large, too, sometimes almost overwhelming, but the poetry waits them out. This poet is in history and therefore dying, but in poetry he is hugely alive: "the tissue sings to sinew, 'passerby . . .' / Dying beside you, I feel the live blood simmer / in my palms and feet, and know I am alive."

Corsons Inlet

If A. R. Ammons had written only the title poem of *Corsons Inlet,* he would have, by this alone, indicated his stature as a poet. It is a microcosm of his work's scope; in it are those distinguishing characteristics that give his poetry its force, flexibility, and that extraordinary combination of form and freedom that is its salient virtue. One of the few invariable characteristics of a first-class poet's work is its ability to create a new poetic world, a world unlike that of any other poet; not glimpses of bits of living originality, not the remodeling of one of the thousand worlds we know—but an authentic, unpredictable, organic world, in which nothing is arranged, into which nothing is arbitrarily introduced, a world living out its own laws and surprises. In his preceding book, *Expressions of Sea Level,* Ammons had already moved into this new world, but its qualities have never been so sharply demonstrated in a single poem.

It is this organic quality of the poetry that makes it an event: the evidence that it will have seasons, renewals, shifts, all functioning under its laws. Like any other world, it is comprised of hard and fluid shapes, of moments of knowledge that hold these shapes in tension; moments of experiencing the point at which the poet is "released from forms, / from the perpendiculars, / straight lines, blocks, boxes, binds / of thought / into the hues, shadings, rises, flowing bends and blends / of sight." The title poem, simple and various on its surface, coils, releases itself, spreads out, recoils with growing power and authority; the poetry is moved by the nature of its world: "you can find / in my

---

A review of *Corsons Inlet,* by A. R. Ammons, from *Baltimore Evening Sun,* 8 July 1965.

sayings, / swerves of action / like the inlet's cutting edge: / there are dunes of motion / organizations of grass, white sandy paths of remembrance / in the over-all wandering of mirroring mind."

This poetry is open poetry: everything is ready to receive, to experience, delicately to register, so that there are always uncontrived surprises and relationships, as in "The Yucca Moth":

. . . .
I raid
        a bloom,
spread the hung petals out,
        and, surprised he's not
a bloom-part, find
a moth inside, the exact color,
the bloom his daylight port or cove:

though time comes
        and goes and troubles
are unlessened,
        the yucca is lifting temples
of bloom: from the night
        of our dark flights, can
we go on to heal, live
        out in white-green shade
the radiant, white hanging day?

Poetry with a scope as large as this often suffers from an emotional deficiency, and it would be easy to assume that these poems, for all their immediacy, show a detachment hostile to emotion. But the reverse is true. The emotional strength of the poetry, underlying every leaf and pebble, is so sustained that it can easily be missed. Mr. Ammons can write a poem as overtly emotional as "Dark Song" or the second of "Two Hymns." But the emotional impact of a poem such as "Corsons Inlet" is only realized with the poem's last line.

Mr. Ammons's rapid ascent in the world of poetry is an extraordinarily heartening phenomenon. His poetry cannot be latched onto any form of protest, exhortation, or the exploitation of any personal predicament. "I am no slave that I / should entertain you, say what you want to hear, . . . / I do not care what you think."

Its now widespread recognition is due to the stuff of which it is made: its interrelation of form and content, the honesty and richness of its working detail, and its total sincerity—the sincerity of a poet who, because he has seen, does not have to fake.

"The Strait" is one of the most remarkable religious poems of recent years, using the images of the oracle, the god, and the reader to achieve its austere and penetrating drama. "Catalyst," a poem about scavengers—"all scavengers are honorable: I love them / all, / will scribble hard as I can for them"—is a perfect example of the short distance, in the world of these poems, from the sordid to the dignified. Life circulates through the work, refreshing and renewing it.

Up to now Mr. Ammons's general tendency has been toward the longer poem, but in this new collection poems such as "Dark Song" show vividly that he is capable of producing a beautifully proportioned short poem:

> Sorrow how high it is
> that no wall holds it
> back: deep
>
> it is that no dam undermines
> it: wide that it
> comes on as up a strand
>
> multiple and relentless:
> the young that are
> beautiful must die; the
>
> old, departing,
> can confer
> nothing.

The fact remains that Mr. Ammons's ability to sustain, line by line, a poem such as "The Strait" or "Corsons Inlet" is the measure of his poetic vitality. The endless discussion of what genuinely constitutes "modern" poetry can scarcely go beyond one simple fact: modern poetry is poetry that is alive. If it is alive, it is also, in the deepest sense, modern. This is very modern poetry.

Stories and "Texts" by Samuel Beckett

"Into what nightmare of thingness am I fallen?" cries the protagonist of Beckett's latest book. This lack of human identity, this sense of some inexplicable and tragic miscarriage between the concept of a human being, unique, responsible, and immortal, and the objectlike mental and physical waif who inhabits Mr. Beckett's caves, tubs, ash cans, boats, and jars, is the core of his work. That work, being the initial and still most powerful voice of the Absurd, continues to dominate a school he had no desire to found.

Mr. Beckett is primarily a poet, and it is the presence of a number of distinct poetic qualities that helps to give a universal quality to work that might be expected to be extremely narrow in scope. In the experience of most readers the circumstances he describes are too bizarre to compel recognition, but the passionate sense of a loss applies with a brutal directness to discussions that have become chronic in our culture.

The portrayal of the distress of the creature unable to identify any creator, any explanation of his predicament, any palliation of the cruelty and brutishness that he finds within himself, is Mr. Beckett's forte. This bears no resemblance to the hopeful findings of the apostles of political or social panaceas. It is closer to the lament of a Job who has lost his religious faith without losing his religious desire. For the Beckett protagonist, to lack any semblance of an answer is to live in hell. Lacking this answer, he feels that he simply ceases to exit, and his humor—bitter,

---

A review of *Stories and Texts for Nothing,* by Samuel Beckett, from *Baltimore Sun,* 25 July 1967.

bawdy, and very, very funny—remains, in his own words, "the long, silent guffaw of the knowing nonexister."

Because Mr. Beckett is a poet, and because his work is of one piece, with a single protagonist under the masks of qualities and circumstances, we find in "texts for nothing" the familiar Beckett properties and touchstones: the shrinking space that traps the protagonist into those containers that are all surrogates for the human skull; the wheels—bicycle, train, carriage wheels—that never cease to turn but never arrive; the wearing sense of an isolation that enforces the composite role of recorder, judge, and criminal in a trial that never ends. "It's tiring—very tiring—in the same breath to record the doom, don the black cap and collapse in the dock." Also, and most important, there is present the obsession with light, the unobtainable but always desired light, which might counteract the darkness of "the long silence"—that silence that has haunted Beckett, Ionesco, and Ingmar Bergman. Mr. Beckett's humor is solidly in the tradition of the great and savage Irish satirists, but often it's warmer and more humanly appealing, with a strong flavor of the music hall and the circus clown.

The texts for nothing are superior to the short stories. Mr. Beckett has done little with the latter form since the early but brilliant "More Kicks than Pricks," and it is the "texts," close in form and quality to his most important and least-read work, his novels, that make this book an important addition to the Beckett oeuvre.

Originally written in French, Mr. Beckett's adopted language, the book has been translated by the author, with the assistance of Richard Seaver on two of the four short stories. It is a short book and perhaps a good place for the neophyte to begin a closer acquaintance with the man who, more than any other, has given to the Theater of the Absurd its grip on the contemporary imagination.

The Felicity of J. D. Salinger

In one of his early stories, "De Daumier-Smith's Blue Period," the major direction of the best of J. D. Salinger's work is foreshadowed—from Holden Caulfield's query to the taxi driver about the winter refuge of the Central Park ducks, to Zooey's blurted confession that he doesn't even feel like going downtown to *lunch* with someone any more unless he thinks there's a good chance it's going to turn out to be Jesus . . . or the Buddha. It is difficult, and perhaps indefensible, to tear them from their organic places, but so important do they seem as an indication of how consistently Salinger has seen the way of his own growth that it will be risked.

> As I was returning . . . after dark, I stopped on the sidewalk and looked into the lighted display window of the orthopedic appliances shop. Then something altogether hideous happened. The thought was forced on me that no matter how coolly or sensibly or gracefully I might one day learn to live my life, I would always, at best, be a visitor in a garden of enamel urinals and bedpans, with a sightless, wooden dummy-deity standing by in a marked-down rupture truss. The thought, certainly, couldn't have been endurable for more than a few seconds.

The writer of this passage has exterminated any facile approach to joy. This vision, in the shop window, is of the world in which Samuel Beckett's prose moves, with a differing but equal horror; it is the world made familiar to us by the best of the literature of despair, which, in its turn, comprises most of

---

From *Commonweal,* 26 February 1960.

our best contemporary writing. And it is this first passage that commands respect for the second—the note of felicity that is Salinger's deepest and rarest gift to us:

> In the nine o'clock twilight . . . there was a light on in the orthopedic appliances shop. I was startled to see a live person in the showcase, a hefty girl of about thirty, in a green, yellow and lavender chiffon dress. She was changing the truss on the wooden dummy. . . . I stood watching her, fascinated, till suddenly she sensed, then saw, that she was being watched. I quickly smiled, to show her that this was a non-hostile figure beyond the window-panes, but it did no good. The girl's confusion was out of all normal proportion. She blushed, she dropped the removed truss, she stepped back on a stack of irrigation basins—and her feet went out from under her. I reached out to her, instantly, hitting the tips of my fingers on the glass. She landed heavily on her bottom, like a skater. She immediately got to her feet without looking at me. Her face still flushed, she pushed her hair back with one hand, and resumed lacing up the truss on the dummy. It was just then that I had my Experience. Suddenly . . . the sun came up and sped toward the bridge of my nose at the rate of ninety-three million miles a second. Blinded and very frightened, I had to put my hand on the glass to keep my balance. The thing lasted for no more than a few seconds. When I got my sight back the girl had gone from the window, leaving behind her a shimmering field of exquisite, twice-blessed enamel flowers.

Salinger has struck his note. The sordid, soulless, hopeless, pointless, has been fractured by the force of the delicate, irresistible infusion: the human exchange of beatific signals. The grotesquely clad, grotesquely occupied girl, separated from the watching boy by every barrier conceivable, has brought down upon him the bolt of revelation. But this moment sternly satisfies the mind. This is no maudlin positive thinking about trusses and ugliness. Nor is it sentimental evasion. The sordidness, in this moment, is not compromised with; it is destroyed.

"I am," says Salinger's protagonist, Buddy Glass, "unjolly, unmerry, to the marrow, but my afflatus seems to be puncture-proof." And Seymour, just before his marriage, writes in his diary: "Oh God, if I am anything by a clinical name I'm a kind of paranoiac in reverse. I suspect people of plotting to make me happy." He has written of the stigmata of joy:

> I have scars on my hands from touching certain people. Once, in the park, when Franny was still in the carriage, I put my hand on the downy pate of her head and left it there too long. Another time . . . with Zooey during a spooky movie. He was about six or seven, and he went under the seat to avoid watching a scary scene. I put my hand on his head. Certain things, certain colors and textures of human hair leave permanent marks on me.

When the creator of characters as sensitive to suffering and forms of evil as are Salinger's can recur to the clear note of joy, and sustain it, something so rare in current literature has occurred that it had better be examined. And a beginning can be made by asking two questions.

First, why have the dominant forces of Salinger's work been bypassed with a nervous rush? Second, through what forms does his sense of joy express itself?

So far, public comment on Salinger's work is like the comments a panic-stricken, valiant, Victorian-minded spinster might make in trying to discuss Dr. Kinsey's report without referring to sex. These critics are interested in Mr. Salinger's modulations of style, in his psychology, in his characterization, in the increasingly vertiginous path he has set himself—but their acknowledgment of the core of his work is absent. Even in *Franny and Zooey*, in which the author's own statement becomes explicit, if characteristic, the religious core is passed off as Salinger's method of proving his biographical or psychological point.

Detractors and admirers alike battle on grounds of a spectacular irrelevance. ("I do cavil," says Buddy ardently, "with . . . the current ruling intellectual aristocracy educated in one or another of the big public psychoanalytical schools. . . . They're a peerage of tin ears.") Salinger's methods, his style, his course, certainly, are extraordinarily interesting, but they are interesting most of all—perhaps, in the last analysis, exclusively—in the framework of an objective followed with an organized and meticulously logical determination. That objective is the pursuit of wisdom, and its core is religious.

One of three most urgent preoccupations underlying the fable of the Glass family (the related stories by which the full stature of Salinger as a writer has been revealed) is that of incarnation; the relevation, through matter, of spirit. The urinals and bedpans, in the blinding sun of Bobby's revelation, became a field of beautiful and twice-blessed enamel flowers.

From here on the list grows: Esmé's watch, bringing sleep to a mind on the brink of disaster; the "perfectly innocent Blake lyric" pinned "like a poultice" to Sergeant X's shirt in the front lines; the little green clothbound book of the Pilgrim that rests on Franny's knees in the ladies' room at Sickler's; the use of Seymour's phone in Zooey's rescue of a floundering Franny—all these are the gift made flesh. This is the substructure of all the Glass stories, shading boundlessly, into Salinger's second foundation, the illusion of classification.

Here, again, the development is not random. Teddy says, at first, he would not have children told how an elephant is big or grass green but learn the classification after experiencing the substance. This is perfected and clarified when the four-year-old girl who tells Buddy she has two boyfriends answers his "What are their names?" with "Bobby and Dorothy"; more overtly, in Zooey's childhood comment on the identical houses in indistinguishable streets: "Zooey said they are 'nice.' He said you'd keep thinking everyone you met was your wife or your mother or father, and people would always be throwing their arms around each other wherever they went and it would look 'very nice.' " The unity essence projected through the distinction in persons.

One of Salinger's special gifts is the juxtaposition of the august and the trivial, in which the latter never deflates the former but is, instead, mysteriously infused by it, while never losing its own nature. The vaudevillian's bicycle, the boy's marble, the shoes shined for the Fat Lady, expand and deepen before our eyes, suddenly congruous. These intimate and unevident relationships are an integral part of the way in which Salinger thinks and writes.

The third foundation of Salinger's work is poetry. A brief, elliptical glimpse of his view of poetry is dropped, as though accidentally, in Seymour's depressed, exalted, quasi-affectionate description of his unnerving mother-in-law to be. He marvels at her courage. She goes here and there, does this and that, when, he says, she might as well be dead. And what is Seymour's analysis of a person who might as well be dead? "A person deprived for life of any understanding or taste for the main current of poetry which flows through things, all things."

Salinger's preoccupation with poetry is intense. "They," Buddy says, "couldn't see Seymour for what he was—a poet, for God's sake." (And here the dependent phrase is not accidental.) "And I mean a poet." "I know this much is all," Franny says. "If you're a poet, you do something beautiful. I mean you're supposed to *leave* something beautiful after you get off the page and everything."

Seymour, the poet, is aware that the path of poetry may cut across another path and veer away in its passage. Seymour sees poetry as at once a manner of life and a crisis—"and poetry surely is a crisis, perhaps the only actionable one we can call our own."

On these bases—matter as incarnation of spirit; the unity of essence, secret under its distinctions; and poetry as an implacable, demanding kind of wisdom—Salinger constructs the dignity of his joy. It is this dignity that is essential, that it be not a substitute, cheap, spurious, full of false claims and lies, but, instead, the pure essence that has nothing to do with satisfactions, content, or even the presence of sorrow; invulnerable to the event. "My afflatus seems to be puncture-proof."

It is a joy based on gratitude, and that gratitude demands the incarnation, essence, and poetry for its justification. It is a joy skillfully and inevitably clothed in contemporaneity, as our despair has been clothed in contemporaneity. This is one of the things that has made Salinger's core difficult. The thought, speech, clothes, setting, the very skin and bones of his people, are passionately of a time, of a moment—a time and moment in which their timelessness and universal energy is released. Zooey *had* to be a television actor, to use midcentury idiom, to live in a New York apartment, in *order* to say:

> Not that anyone's interested, but I can't even sit down to a goddam *meal,* to this day, without saying the Four Great Vows under my breath. . . . My God, I've been mumbling that under

> my breath three meals a day every day of my life since I was ten. I can't *eat* unless I say it. I tried skipping it once, when I was having lunch with LeSage. I gagged on a goddam cherrystone clam doing it.

The theme of gratitude recurs. Zooey struggling not to make a misstep, during Franny's crisis, argues with his mother and himself:

> For a psychoanalyst to be any good with Franny at all, he'd have to be a pretty peculiar type. I don't know. He'd have to believe that it's through the grace of God that he has the native intelligence to be able to help his goddam patients at *all* . . . if she got somebody . . . who didn't even have any crazy, mysterious, *grat*itude for his insight and intelligence—she'd come out of an analysis in even worse shape than Seymour did.

The student of Salinger's work receives a gift—a gift that he may or may not value or decide to accept. In order to hear Salinger there must be more suspension of disbelief than has often been accorded him. He himself has shown his consciousness of this in his prefatory remarks on Seymour: those who are unwilling or unable to listen can get off here. Those who accept his offering will, in turn, and inevitably, offer gratitude.

III

Travel and Op-Ed Pieces

Atlantic City Glowed like a Jewel

When I was a small child, Atlantic City glowed like a jewel in my mind. At the time of the First World War we spent an entire winter there; I cannot imagine why. Now that it is becoming the East's response to Las Vegas, that jewel is small and remote but nevertheless bright.

I loved it most dearly. We lived in the Dennis Hotel, and, never having stayed very long anywhere, I settled into its joys freely. On bright days the whole shining outside world, bisected by the boardwalk, waited. Up that boardwalk my nurse and I trudged steadfastly. Our ultimate destination was the Japanese ping-pong tables far down, almost at the opposite end. I had twenty cents a day, which entitled me to two full games, with their accumulating points, which a high-spirited Japanese in a gray felt hat noted down scrupulously in a giant ledger. On the shelves behind him radiated prizes to be earned: Japanese dolls with chalky faces and straight thick black hair above their brilliant kimonos; tea sets, lustrous in rose and green; bookends, gnarled and loaded with colored fruits (I still have a pair earned by enormous columns of figures), on and on in rainbow rows. I became skillful. "Come hundred!" cried my Japanese scorer, hanging over the bulbous rounded end of the table, and sometimes, indeed, the round wooden ball wallowed in the hundred hole, wallowed and settled. More often, wallowed, shot out, and rolled aimlessly against the six-inch side. There was a sinking feeling as the final ball of the second dime left my fingers.

But then there was the red-topped Garden Pier, in whose

From *Baltimore Sun,* 21 November 1978.

USO I saw two melancholy sailors, their starched white caps thrust back on their heads, stepping seriously and clumsily together to a tinny *Ja-da, Jada* (ja-da, jada, jing, jing, jing). There was the window where the saltwater taffy (which I was not allowed to eat) was pulled slowly and taffily apart by a shiny machine—mint green, chocolate, dark peach colored—and reappeared in cylindrical, bullet-like offerings encased in paper twists on which appeared the name of its species. There was Child's window, in which a white-capped muscular man tossed up and caught on a spatula cakes that browned, bubbling a little, on a built-in grill. And auction palaces, in whose windows lamps shone by daylight and soft, thick rugs richly glowed. These marvelous places we never entered, like all the out-of-pocket, conscious of our irrelevance, but we stood for minutes on end, watching the fortunate on rows of folding chairs over which rugs were cast, with money for Oriental rugs, brass lamps, and rooms in which to put them.

We were familiar with all the piers—the Steel Pier, illustrated by a lady in pink tights riding a plunging horse through the air into a small tank; the Fun House, which I was forbidden to enter, its having been condemned as vulgar. I did forlornly, beyond the stick fence, watch the lucky ladies entering the Wind Tunnel, their skirts soaring like umbrellas, rolling and screaming in the Barrel; bucking violently on the Bucking Bridge. I could see just one distorted figure in the Funny Mirrors section.

Up and down, cleaving to the bank of narrow, straight-laid boards stretched on each side of the broad cross-boards of the boardwalk, wider set with glimpses of cold, disordered sand between their gaps, went the shining, shellacked yellow of the chairs, each with its curled wicker prow, each with its toiling pusher, head bent, feet rhythmic. Hypochondriacs and other eccentrics could be spotted by the monstrous glass superstructure, which sheltered them from the air's salt.

Down the beach, elbows flapping, sea air clearly visible below their buttocks at each stride, rode the equestrians of the beach. The luckless horses waiting their turns were covered by plaid throws; the pony carts, as yellow as the chairs, were moored by a great round weight at a strap's end. Next to the horse stand, the Beach Artist had his immense bank of solidified sand on which appeared his major work of the week. Below it, close to the scratched and pegged canvas spotted with coins, he worked on his more ephemeral portraits—a little girl, her round felt hat one sharp circle, her sand pigtails clear; a young man with wavy hair shooting in jerky lines on the sand canvas.

By the time the sun set fire to the Traymore windows, making it into a medieval castle burning on the winter sky, there had been almost too much to absorb.

On rainy days there was the Dennis Library: I went straight through Robert Service and Zane Grey. The latter has not stayed with me, except as a vague aura of sagebrush, though I do remember my hot annoyance when an adult laughed at me—after questioning me in the uninterested manner of adults about what I was reading—when I said, *The Up Trail.* I can recite, endlessly, verses beginning "They're making my money diminish / I'm sick of the taste of champagne / Thank God when I'm skinned to the finish / I'll pipe for the Yukon again." Or "Out of the night which was thirty below / And into the din and the glare / There stumbled a miner, fresh from the creek / Dog-dirty and loaded for bear."

There was an uncomprehended excitement. The only thing clear to me was that I was intensely patriotic. I knitted yards and yards of thick khaki rows for mufflers: on slippery small needles I knitted string into lumpy white washcloths with some horrible kind of cotton thread. It never struck me as improbable that the soldiers would scrub their shining faces with them each morning. I eagerly attended bond rallies, manned from a tank hoisted onto the boardwalk.

Sometimes, pushing open the huge resisting glass door to the seaside balcony that terminated each hall, I stepped out into a different world. It was always deserted, the rails of the metal staircases that connected balcony to balcony cold with blown winter spray, the sea dark and noisy, the sense of isolation sudden and startling. That was the time when ships were sinking, when Dachshunds were stoned in American cities, when Kriesler was refused permission to give a concert. I did not know these things until later. But, when I stepped out onto the winter balcony from the heat of the hotel, I did know that something was changed.

In my mind's eye only can I locate them now—the ping-pong scorer, the flapjack man, the chair pushers, the riders, of that Atlantic City.

Never Was the Play the Thing

Years ago the Palace ceased to be. For the benefit of those so luckless as not to know, the Palace was to the world of vaudeville, what the role of Hamlet is to the actor, Everest to the mountaineer. From the cities and boondocks all over America, dwindled, thinned out again finally, a small dazzling band of survivors achieved the Dream: an engagement at the Palace.

If a great event in one's life is that which leaves a rich, glowing, permanent legacy, then my debut as a member of the Palace's audience, when I was eleven years old, was a major event. My brother, who was eleven years older, took me, one Saturday afternoon, for the first of a series of peerless occasions. Not only did the setting of that stage frame the greatest Oriental acrobats, the suavest magicians, the most breathtaking dance teams, but there, wafted to that summit, without the long and painful ascent, appeared the great stars. It was from gilt chairs of the right-hand lower box (stage left) that I first saw Ethel Barrymore, Cyril Maude, Nazimova; that a special sort of communion—one of freedom from the limits of identity, of generosity and breathless collaboration that has never left me—established itself. Though I remember, with grateful delight, the flowerlike ladies of the human pyramid, the magician's servant-nymph, that absolutely magic sound—soft, slurred, perfectly complex—the sound of a flawless soft-shoe team, it was the actors who revolutionized my consciousness.

Instantly, and completely, I knew that I was also performing, in a complex collaboration—that the instant of identity that we created was something unique to that place, that moment, never

---

From *Baltimore Sun,* 6 June 1978.

to be identically repeated. I hadn't yet been told by actors, "Each audience is different," but I knew what these actors and that audience had made between them.

This consciousness set the movies—my secondary love—forever in their place, however ingenious intelligent, and even superior, the competition might be. True, I went to the movies whenever I possibly could. Part of my personal life were Conrad Nagel in a pit of crocodiles (*why?*); Gloria Swanson, sleek and boyish in a rakish cap, as a jewel thief; Wallace Reid, boyish in an air of ingenuousness and a sweater. Twice I saw John Gilbert spill hot soup on Mae Murray's dress (my French schoolmate, with swift Gallic intuition hissed in my ear, "Il l'a fait exprés!"), but never, never was it the same. All this had been done, long ago and far away, before the mechanical eye of the camera; cut and edited.

But Jane Cowl, clinging to her bombarded switchboard, plugging in crucial messages as all crumbled; John Barrymore's fiendish beauty, in "The Jest"; George Arliss, turbaned and tiger-smooth in the "Green Goddess"—these were another matter. There are worse supplements to the adolescent diet than corn and ham. I have forgotten many a book, many an acquaintance, many an event—but never Ethel Barrymore (in God knows what), bedeviled by debt, betrayed in love, leaning wearily back on a gilded sofa, the invisible stringed orchestra playing her request; how after swallowing in her demitasse a perfectly painless poison, she drew off, with what infinite grace, her final ring, and, placing it on the unpayable check as the waiter bent courteously above her, murmured to me, to me, "Tell them they can stop the music—now."

Feeling that Leslie Howard was teaching me all I knew, or ever needed to know, emotionally, I saw *Outward Bound* six times, as pocket money permitted, from a series of seats gradually retreating from the stage, until Leslie Howard and Margo Gilmore, as the suicidal lovers rescued by their dog, became, from close under the theater's gilded roof, the loveliest of specks to my straining eye.

Never, never, was the play the thing. Then, and now, the thing was and is the living moment created by actor and audience, momentary, unpreservable, unique. With the houselights up, in the crowded aisle, I can wince from failure with the most acid critic. From sad experience I avoid reading interviews with actors as I would avoid watching a swan take a stroll. But, once we are in our proper places, from our respective positions, we reach across the footlights and create our joint moment of truth.

Computers, microfilm, audiovisual experience, will reveal possibilities I can barely imagine. But nothing, absolutely nothing, can threaten that electric contact, that almost physical union, in which flesh-and-blood human beings, now, at this moment, tell us and show us and ask us to believe. And fondly, naively, I believe that we are indispensable—that no canned laughter can substitute for that risky, moment-to-moment collaboration. The magician's trick may fail; the actor may blank out; someone in the audience may faint. Maybe no one will laugh—maybe there won't be that special stretched hush at the climactic scene. It is not settled. It is alive. It has not been packaged.

At the Palace I was never quite sure what was going to happen. I am not sure now, as the lights go up. What I am is grateful; what I do is wait, one more time, to find out.

Happily in Transit, Transported

All of us know enough to equate the wheel with a leap in progress. But, for a long time, with what happy slowness it revolved, according to the nature of ox, mule, or horse. Now, after thousands of years, what options snatch us away.

I am patsy for them all; I like to be transported. Often, when people say they like to travel, they mean, very reasonably, that they like to see and explore beautiful or exotic or just different places, away from those in which they habitually struggle. But often they detest the means of getting there and attempt constantly to evade, reduce, or outwit them. Besides its handsome face and overpowering presence, what is the Concorde's chief seduction (to those seduced, that is)? The fact that its passengers will be in the vehicle for the shortest conceivable time.

I enjoy the physical process of travel, and no amount of sitting in an airport while "engine trouble" is dealt with; of riding in trains in which the heating system has freaked out, leaving me sweating or shivering; no number of times in which, in isolated purlieus, the small malignant red eye of trouble has opened on my dashboard; not even the obsessional loquacity of taxi drivers, can root out my unreasoning joy. I love the process of being taken from where I am to somewhere else. This may be evidence of an insensate optimism or just a congenital restlessness. I never buy a train ticket without a lift of heart. My enthusiasm, battered but living, has survived the change from white napery, crested china, and a cordial hovering to the lank cheese between the powdery slices and the paper cup's contents, sloshing

---

From *Baltimore Sun,* 22 August 1979.

as the train bucks and switches, consumed propped against the littered bar.

No longer can one read happily in transit, as wheels hurtle over ancient tracks at space-age speed. I have ridden in total darkness; propped my feet from oozing water (a broken pipe?); once, the icy week of Jimmy Carter's Inauguration, stood patiently while the personnel struggled to release frozen doors so that I could, after all, get off in Baltimore. They got the doors open, all right, but the steps were frozen more securely, and we had to hurl ourselves down into the game but horrified grip of a conductor and a brakeman, calling encouragement from below. I flew through the air, carrying a large purse and a small briefcase. It was my nearest approach to free fall.

Nothing is really dear to humans that does not need to be defended, especially against accurate attack. I have no adequate defense of the wheel: it is not so ancient nor so majestic as the prow. It is earthbound, and neither sea nor air will have it. It is a weapon and menace. It is prolific as the rabbit and bigger and faster. It is an object of desire to adolescence and of fear to old age. But, from the spokes under the covered wagons dangerously creating a continent, to those turning slowly on the cart, in the first days of spring, carrying the call, "Strawberries! Fresh straaw-berr-ries!" what hasn't it had to offer? Its ruts are in the paving of Pompeii; it bounces the beach buggy over the barren spaces of the moon.

Taxi drivers, I am convinced, suffer from the obsessive loneliness of a human being constantly exposed to others to whom he, like his wheel, is an object of utility. Either passengers wish to talk together, or, like me, they crave with intensity a patch of silence in the loud pattern of the day. But the taxi driver, pent and penned, subject to idiot drivers, fishy-eyed cops, lunatic pedestrians, and his own unsolved problems, with plenty of time for brooding, has a ravening hunger for communication. Taxi drivers are by nature hortatory; they are tireless explainers. They have theories on major subjects—women drivers, drunken drivers (small choice there), city ordinances, mayors, traffic czars. But they have, too, more personal concerns: minor domestic problems (how solved or not solved); special health diets; previous passengers who should never have been picked up in the first place. The current passenger leaves the cab feeling that his own burdens are, after all, lighter than he had supposed.

And, though the voice and the meter tick on, I am pleased to be that passenger. Stalled in New York's garment district at 2 P.M.; grazing the pillars of the elevated (as a New York child I learned not to close my eyes during this process, a supremely useful conditioning); sliding on paralyzed wheels down the icy surface of my unsalted, unashed Baltimore hill—the arms of transportation are around me. They affect me with an insensate optimism.

This explains, I suppose, why a plane's take-off has a miraculous excitement; its descent a taint of disappointment, as the flying object sprouts wheels and bumps on tarmac. I know nothing quite like that first transformation: what seems at first the stealthy movement of the terminal across the thick glass of the pane, the gathering speed as the wheels thunder along, the defiance of gravity as the huge weight climbs and lifts into air, and the *chock* that signifies that wheel has given up its function, wheel is wing. Beyond the glass is a world of great curling crests, towers and turrets of cloud terrain; a world of lovely, unreliable shapes. Nothing stales its variety, not even the bored, conscientious stewardess, gesturing toward the exits, hauling out the oxygen mask. Even the whistle, provided me "to attract attention" should I be plunged into the February Atlantic waters, cannot dim me. Shall I envision myself, like a frantic doorman, shrilly hailing taxis at the dinner hour? No, I have what I want. At the moment, earth left below, destination in abeyance, I am, in every sense, transported.

A Kind of Beginning

Beginnings are wonderful and discouraging things. Wonderful, because without them old disappointments, failures, disillusions, would clog the days; discouraging, because, like most things, they don't stay uninjured for very long.

Christmas, the traditional or religious celebration, is a date we have arbitrarily set upon the calendar, but it is, too, always a beginning, something still fresh, unflawed, the image of which is birth.

The big bang that traditionally (and often pretty heavy-handedly) goes along with our celebration of New Year's certainly isn't for the marvelous things we've done, changes we've made, stupidities we've avoided, in the preceding twelve months; it's for the arbitrary, person-made marker we've set in the calendar to say that here we have decided that something is finished, and something we haven't yet had a chance to spoil is about to start. And it requires the sense of continuity, of other years past and future, to have its special meaning.

To spend Christmas or New Year's away from the entire structure of labeled seasons, of prescribed activity, is in itself a kind of beginning, in which the isolated person is conscious of two kinds of time: the immense stretch of the enormous past; and the divisions of month, and days, and hours, in which human beings move, checking off recognizable and familiar sections of the year.

I spent the minutes just before and after dawn on Christmas morning sitting quietly in a jeep, under a thorn bush, waiting for the sun. That was several years ago, according to my personal

From *Baltimore Sun,* 21 November 1977.

calendar, but what we were looking at showed almost no arbitrary division from what I might have seen if it had been a hundred or five hundred years ago; nothing to say, today is Christmas.

It was supposed to be the dry season in Kenya, but it had fooled everyone—there had been lots of rain. And now, as the dark began to have that thinness that means something bright is coming, we began to see, a few hundred yards away, a little pool, formed from rainwater collected in a dip in the wide plain; an oval of pallor, a faint glitter. On the far side of its small surface two shapes began to form, first dark, then pale, and, finally, of palest gold—a lion and a lioness.

They stood side by side, drinking. The pool hadn't been there before, and again it wouldn't be there, but it was there now, and with their great triangular cats' heads lowered, they drank, close together, with a lapping sound.

All of a sudden, color arrived. The plain turned the same dusty gold as the lions, a transfusion of blue seeped into the sky, and the blue, and a white small irregular cloud, were reflected in the pool, where two other lions appeared, drinking, muzzle to muzzle with the stooping pair.

Then the lions in air, the lions in water, lifted their heads, first the lion, then the lioness. They stood for a moment motionless above their motionless images, staring off into the great brightening distance. Then easily, the legs pacing smoothly as pistons, the heads stretched a little forward, they moved away; they passed into the high tawny grasses and melted; and there was nothing left in the pool but the blue sky and the sun that would suck it up.

It was beginning, a new day. Christmas was there.

A week later, on New Year's Eve, we went to bed very early, at the foot of Kilimanjaro. We had been traveling by jeep all day, and we had had a modest celebration at our camp dinner, and we were very tired.

The evening was heavily clouded, with a thick mist, and Kilimanjaro, from two-thirds up its black bulk, was totally invisible. Though we had been told that this was more usual than not, it was exasperating to know that the snows were there, the huge peak somewhere, in the sort of cloud bank common enough anywhere. No story Hemingway or anyone else ever wrote has a more magic name than "The Snows of Kilimanjaro," and we had to go to sleep with just that name.

Someone knocked hastily on the door much later—the flashlight showed ten minutes to twelve. It was our fifteen-year-old companion from the next cabin. Hurry, he said, hurry, hurry.

We dragged blankets around us and walked into the cold air. Somewhere, high up, winds had moved things about. No cloud, no mist; under the huge African moon stood Kilimanjaro, naked, brilliant. "Happy New Year," we said to each other.

The Meaning of Arrival

When you go away to distant places, you are supposed to know about certain things when you come back—the museums, the architecture, the form of government, the best shopping areas, the best restaurants.

Without for an instant denigrating the importance of these areas of information (on which I comment with as little provocation as the next traveler), again and again I find that what really sticks with me most permanently from a visit to a new country, what lingers as the most intense flavor of that experience, is a person or an event—a person whom I may have seen only for a moment and whose name I will never know or an event, sometimes small, quickly over, without practical benefit, which is so tinctured with the essence of the place that afterward that person, that moment, becomes a sort of quintessence. If you remember such things of a place with sentimentality, if you say to yourself, "That is how the place always is. It is like that," they will shrivel up and change into something to throw away.

I remember good and varied things about Tanganyika—but, most sharply, I remember crawling about on my hands and knees, on sunny stubble, in hot fragrant air, struggling to reassemble the contents of a vial of pink-and-white antibiotics, while two manic monkeys danced above me on a bougainvillea-covered roof.

I had stayed behind in our game preserve compound while everyone else had gone off to photograph lions or, with a bit of extra luck, a leopard or cheetah. I was ailing, my husband had just recovered, and we were sharing an antibiotic, under the

---

From *Baltimore Sun,* 20 October 1977.

usual threat of what would befall us if we stopped in mid-treatment. At four o'clock had come a welcome tea tray. I could see in the distance thorn trees and acacias; the sky stretched over great African space, and it was all fresh and strange. I sat there on the little concrete porch—drinking my tea, the antibiotics beside my tray—in a daze of convalescent content. A little way off two small monkeys materialized and turned worried eager furry faces on me as I feasted.

"Never leave food on the porch," I had been warned, and so, under their eyes, I took in my tray, leaving the vial, colorful as a flower but no sandwich, as was immediately noted. A violent clatter; then whoops of malignant joy. Up swooped my monkeys, up the bougainvillea vine to the roof, clutching the vial. Did *they* have trouble with the cap? The answer was a shower of colored capsules, wide and far, into the vines, over the roof, onto the stubble.

Intimidated child of science, I knelt humbly, prying apart grass blades, crawling erratically as I spied a hint of pink, while the children of instinct watched me from above, chattering with satisfaction. I can still see the small leaping figures, my own laborious silly fingers, searching, retrieving, and smell the hot stubble and the flowers' breath, as the high simians marveled at the creeping monster below.

And I remember many good and varied things about Guatamala, but a grim hour there remains the most I have learned of traveler's comfort.

For dull reasons we crossed the border from Mexico to Guatamala far later than intended. No one had told us that few motorists care to drive themselves up the road to Chichicastenango, even by daylight. It was already in Guatamala's sudden dusk that we found the small turn-off, and in minutes we were in blackness, climbing a mountain road so narrow what could pass? Round and round and round, up and up and up, it went, higher and higher, darker and darker.

We had driven all day, part of it where there had been washouts, through gullies and over crushed rock, and we were tired, and we began to think we were lost, too. There had been a sign, where we started up, but now there was absolutely no trace of human existence. Shelters, market stalls by the roadside, in the brief glance of the headlights, looked deserted. Down the great slopes of the mountain not one light showed. The road had got so steep that it felt as though the car were climbing a wall, and then a huge moon lifted itself, and all *below* us lay the peaks of mountains, as though we were alone above a distant earth.

Could we turn back? Not possibly. Could we creep cautiously? Each curve had become so steep that we had to rush it for fear the car would stall at a nearly perpendicular angle. There seemed to be no time, no distance. Just cold blackness and another dark almost perpendicular curve and the great somber mountains.

Then, unbelievably, there was one faint, far point of light: a lamp somewhere, somewhere above us. It was improbable, but it was there. Around another towering curve—a string of lights, trembling a little as lights do in the night air.

A street, a blaze of light, an inn; lights, lights, masses of flowers. Two men in brilliant costumes, smiling, raising their hands, opening the car door. No wayfarer in any tale, no Walter Scott horseman on a sleety night, no Thomas Hardy heath traveler in a storm, ever understood more blessedly the meaning of arrival.

A red-tiled floor, a gigantic fire, a huge bed, a tray with steaming coffee. And far away, somewhere down in the valley, the sound of a wooden flute, chaining faint wandering notes.

Before we slept we stood for a moment at the window; the moon still was high, and the flute notes, carrying so far in the huge silence, came up from someone, playing for his own, or someone else's, pleasure.

Where the Wild Went About

We seem to be incorrigibly anthropomorphic, having an unquenchable desire to make the nonhuman over into our form, no matter how ludicrous or depressing the result. The strange—the Other—fascinates us; the rarer the life form, the more we prize it. But steadily, heavily, we try to feed our egos by forcing the wild to become tame.

For a long time that didn't particularly matter. Dogs, horses, and the local zoo could give us our garbled version of the life of the beasts; still there were jungle and tundra, riverbanks and mountains, where the wild went about its wordless ways. But now that wildness is draining and shrinking.

The animals play a huge part in our myths and language; like shamans, we extract a characteristic we assume to be typical and attribute it to ourselves. Someone is "brave as a lion" (though a male lion's outstanding characteristic is sloth), "gentle as a dove" (which is a cannibal), or has "the memory of an elephant" (though it now turns out the elephant may be as forgetful as you and I).

We put the bear to dance and place the bull in our metaphorical china shop. (Only the giraffe—the warped triangle of its mild face cruising shyly through leafy branches—seems to have escaped our simile.)

We know perfectly well that the dancing bear is a zombie in bearskin. We know that the tiger pursed up on the big ball has lost his nature. What we don't seem to realize is how horrible it will be when and if he ceases to burn bright in Blake's night forests.

From *Baltimore Sun,* 12 June 1980.

It is the wildness that is irreplaceable. It is the wildness that separates the wolf from the trimmed and clipped and altered dog or the mustang from the third at Pimlico or the junk man's locomotion.

Perhaps our sentimentality is worse than our ferocity; animals, after all, comprehend pain, defeat, and battle. But they have yet to conceive the notion of having us feed their egos by poorly imitating them.

We crave strangeness; the shrinking jungles and inaccessible spots of earth still haunt us. But let us lay hands on the earthly wild, and, if we do not skin it or mount its head, we tame it. It is a viewing object or a pet. It is no accident that the adjectives *strange* and *wonderful* are linked. "A wonderful piece of luck," we say, but what we first meant was something to wonder at, something full of wonder. Wonder seems to be not just threatened but close to extinct.

Obviously, we are going to have our dogs, our cats, our horses. Certainly, our zoos have become vital. But we might also remember that these denizens of our parks, stables, and houses are the remotest and most shabby-genteel of their kind, a sort of strayed species, caught in never-never land, where they are neither free in their first nature nor the equals of their tamers and owners. The closer they come to being a ludicrous human instead of a capable beast, the more confused and harried their gaze becomes. (The glass-brown gaze of a small capuchin monkey on a leash peers into the visitor's eyes with a look just short of speech. But it does not speak.)

In Tobago, the wild parrots of Bloody Bay fly in pairs so high they are lost against the sun. But we have managed to extract a plea for a cracker from the beak of their cousin. We can ride cycles better than a bear, walk upright better than a dog (Dr. Johnson knew all about that), ride a pony better than a lion. But what fun to savor the superiority we demonstrate while the beasts, clumsy and inept, parody us.

In a splendid poem, Auden speaks of the great herds of reindeer flowing over the arctic tundra "silently and very fast." Not only do we have Rudolph the red-nosed reindeer, but he's submitted to one of the most repulsive of human reactions. Rudolph, alas, was a pariah, vilified and ostracized. His problem is that he isn't permitted "to play in any reindeer games." Then the boss invited the lowly clerk to dinner: the prince nods to the obscure courtier. Santa picks Rudolph as reindeer-of-the-year; he will lead the sleigh. Says the song in nine thousand repetitions, "Then how the reindeer loved him!" Oh degenerate reindeer! "Success," remarked John Kennedy, "has a hundred parents; failure is an orphan." But *reindeer?*

Well, populations will multiply, farms will and must erode game preserves. Nowadays when we say "Alaska" we think "oil." Nothing is going to reverse the clock's motion. But, while we still have a few thousands of fellow inhabitants on a globe shrinking like a leaking balloon, let us still draw delight, as long as we can, from the thought of the wild—the elephant herds swaying and shifting at the water hole; the moonlit leopard on the tree trunk; the lioness sunk in the hot grasses in a nest of cubs.

The Swamp's Talk

We are told it is the zoo that soon will be the last refuge of wild animal life. Already several endangered species are safest there. With all its warts the zoo image is an invaluable one: where else shall an urban generation, for whom the animal kingdom is represented by the cat, the dog, and the sparrow, watch the huge, ill-fitted, moss-gray hide of a looming elephant, or the slanted spring of the giraffe's neck carrying the long, gentle face, the paintbrush lashes?

The masses of the human majority gather round the cage of the solitary or paired captive. People flow like an uncertain river around the rails and bars, the pits and the ledges, where the wordless minority returns their stares or ignores them.

Most of us live in areas in which the human animal is in such an overwhelming majority that, for us, the status of the minority, of intrusion into a world where we are vastly outnumbered, is almost inconceivable. And yet there are travelers for whom no museum, no architecture, no shards of history made visible, are so transforming, so curiously liberating, as that exact experience.

The snowy egrets and the scarlet ibis fly home to roost at night in the branches of the mangroves, on islets in the Caroni Swamp, outside Port of Spain. Late in the afternoon a small boat snarls down the long, narrow canal toward the giant swamp. Always the mangroves advance to close in the boat, with a sidelong thrust of their crooked branches, a motion invisible. Past great tumuli, some taller than a tall man—the metropolises of the ants—the boat rips along with a steady droning snarl. Then, suddenly, you are in the swamp.

From *Baltimore Sun,* 11 October 1978.

It is no swamp at all but an expanse of shallow lake, no deeper than a foot or so, with canals branching out in a deceptive dozen directions. Small or larger islands of mangroves dot its pale pewter shimmer. The sun is low now. The boat, its motor shut off, slips in close to an island, knocking softly against the mangrove roots, and there is complete silence, until it is torn by another boat, which drones in and hushes beside a distant island.

Spontaneously, no one speaks. The canals stretch out, shining and identical. The sky is still a clear blue, and, against it, two white shapes wing in, curve, and drop into the dark confusion of mangroves. They shine against the leaves' dark, fly up, settle again. Now a flock—twenty? more?—appear, flying fast. They dip, in some preconcerted pattern, rise, dive, and settle. Two mysteriously peel off and sail, zeroing in on a special tree, apart. Now the sky, gradually altering its blue, is full of white wings. The branches of the mangroves grow globes of egrets; one great tree is white with a snowfall of folded wings.

Then, suddenly, very high, directly in the slanted sunlight so that they catch fire against the blue, two scarlet ibis are overhead. They are so bright they dazzle.

Into an uninhabited tree down they drop, and, following them, larger and larger flocks, small and dark in the distance, blazing in the low angle of the sun, they fold into mangroves that now look like giant flame trees in bloom.

Then, with belated pairs and trios still caught and kindled by the sun, a sound begins—confused, rumorous, coming from no special place.

It is some sort of avian congress, a hoarse, muffled speech, not conveying tranquillity or its opposite—concerned with matters specifically nonhuman. It swells and spreads, dies and resumes. The human listener is suddenly conscious of eavesdropping—queer species that she represents: present, uninvited, and invisible, in a city of organized, social, nonhuman life.

All around, the hoarse voices talk, overtaking one another, raucously rising, sinking to a sort of harsh mutter.

Two egrets flash up into the darkening air, find another tree. One cannot say, "a difference of opinion," "a wish for more privacy." This is the inscrutable, blessedly nonverbal world. It is the swamp's talk, the motion and sound of the society of ibis and egret.

All at once, Snarl! A motorboat has started up. Another, and another, from unseen points close to the tiny islands. It is hard to describe the physical sense of shock. It is like being pitched down the well of centuries. The sun has left the swamp; the pewter-colored water has gone dark. Now we are in a line: back along the canal, between the mangrove fingers. No one wants much to speak. The dock is waiting and, after the dusty drive, the lights and noises of Port of Spain: its carnival preparations, its steel bands and calypso tents. At night no one is allowed in the swamp, except government boats, patrolling for poachers, who always manage a boatload of still-warm feathers each night, in the swamp's deep reaches.

No one will be there to see the first light, the earliest sun that will start a stirring, a multiple shifting, and the first hoarse, confident voices, the sound spreading and growing; or the first wings lift into the air.

More White than Feathers

Perhaps because Haiti was the first Caribbean island that I ever saw, it seemed to me beautiful with an almost unreal beauty.

I had been high, high in the hills above Port-au-Prince, above Petionville, above even Kenscoff; and very tired indeed, I was lying back in the battered taxi coming down, down, down. Outside a tiny village—not really even a village—a child came running after the cab. He had on ragged blue pants, and he was cocoa colored and running very fast. He held in his hand a strict, circular bouquet, and the driver slowed doubtfully, muttering. The boy caught up with the cab and grabbed the door at the open window, thrusting the flowers at me with a fierce hope.

"Belles fleurs!" he cried at me, "Jolies! Jolies!" thrusting out his other small hand, a curved scar on its palm. The bouquet was amazingly sophisticated, a formal series of circles, delicately graded in color, with a red tight rosebud at its center. I rummaged rapidly. Not a coin left, nothing whatsoever except the rumpled note for my long drive. The driver, appealed to as the child's eyes went from face to face, was, theoretically, penniless. I held up my empty open coin purse, babbling shamefacedly, "Oui, oui, tellement jolies. Je regrette, je regrette beaucoup." We stared at each other.

The small intense face clouded, the hand with the curved scar pulled back, as the driver lurched into first and around the curve. A moment later, circling lower across the stony ground, the boy came, running harder. My nerves tightened, and I tried to glare. He caught almost up with the cab creaking downhill in second. A great smile flashed out, like a light. "Voila!" he cried,

---

From *Baltimore Sun,* 1 November 1977.

and took aim and, by skill or luck or miracle, threw the bouquet squarely into my lap. On went the cab, picking up speed. I leaned out, waving the bouquet. A small dark hand went into the air and circled in royal gesture.

It is true that strangeness is a part of impact. Subtly but steadily, often familiarity increases knowledge as perception fades.

I was waiting for a bus, in downtown St. Georges, in Grenada. The Grenadan climate is just about perfect; but if, a northerner, you insist on going downtown to the hottest streets, at high noon, the sun you have come so far to meet responds by pouring down upon you in a blast of tropic fervency. I had been tramping up and down all morning, and I was boiling gently, like a muted tea kettle. Beside me, pressed against a wall, angling for inches of shade, was also waiting an old woman; tall, stringy-thin, black, dignified, with an open-work straw hat on her sensible head, close to my stupid bare one. We had smiled at each other, feebly flapping our hands before our faces to stir the air.

Then, "You do come from Canada?" she said to me.

"No," I said, "From the States."

"From California?"

"From Maryland."

"Mary Land," she repeated. "Is it cold?"

"Not very," I said. "Colder than this, I mean . . ."

But she was leading up to something. We bored into a slice of shade. Sweating passersby gleamed like seals.

"You have seen snow?" she said.

"Oh yes," I said. "Often. We have it in lots of places."

She looked at me, her eyes bright as blackberries. "I did see it, in pictures, and like that. In a picture, it was whiter than sand."

"Well, yes," I said. (When it first falls.)

"Or feathers? More white than feathers?"

"Well, it shines, you know."

"Lying on the ground, and so?"

"Yes, and in the air."

"On the ground," she repeated, "It does lie right on the ground, after it fall?"

"Yes, on the ground."

"You have stepped on it?" she said. "You have walked, right on it? Right on over it?"

Have you seene but a bright Lillie grow,
Before rude hands have touch'd it?
Ha' you marked but the fall o'the snow,
B'efore the soyle hath smutched it?

But Ben Jonson had never shown it to me so sudden, and so brilliant.

"Yes," I said, somehow ashamed, like someone who had missed her chance. "I've walked right over it."

There was a huge yellow lurch; it was the bus.

She got on in front of me, her thin muscled legs shining with sweat. She sat down ahead, next to a plump American in a Hawaiian shirt. In a moment she turned her face, and finding mine, gave me a sharp, bright, marveling smile.

The Traveler

Tourists are held in universal obloquy. "I don't want to look like . . ." "The place has gotten to be full of . . . ," etc., etc. Small wonder, since the peculiar is lost, as usual, to the general.

To the sound of a captive steel band, constrained to play, at every single landing, "All Day, All Night, Mary Ann," they are disgorged from the launch onto the lovely crescent of our beach. Gelatinous ladies, to whom adolescence is the dimmest of memories, waddle past, the rims of their bikinis deeply lost. Loud-voiced gentlemen, debouched from a cruise whose price would cause an oil baron to blanch, haggle knowingly over twenty-five cents in the not-at-all certain purchase of a shirt suspended from the knobby fingers of an old woman. Or the chummy type who isolates a native for conversation: one stands over a young man with glazed eyes who leans against a palm bole. The passerby can hear the untiring tones of the vintage bore.

We, of course, are not tourists. We spend a month or two on the island, know its forests and streams, where its monkeys still linger, and where and when the great nets bring in the fish. On the other hand, at what exact point we graduated from tourist to semiresident is cloudy. For our friends who come for two weeks share this sense of superiority. And in a hotel a little way up the beach there is a large room, its glass doors discreetly curtained, their gold letters reading "Residents' Lounge." This distinguishes those guests who stay overnight from prowlers on the launch. I remember sitting proudly in such a lounge in Kenya, a book on my lap, hoi polloi bound for Treetops chattering in five languages on the terrace. So the distinction fades to a needle's point.

From *Baltimore Sun,* 11 October 1979.

The word *traveler,* on the contrary, inspires respect, even envy. The two words have a mutual antipathy. Much have I *toured* in the realms of gold? Never. Why the instinctive feeling of disparity? Because *traveler* suggests exploration, mystery; brings with it the shadow of Ulysses and Marco Polo? As *resident* suggests knowledge, so *traveler* suggests adventure.

Perhaps that is why one thinks of traveling, never of touring, in books. Traveling, in books, is apt to be an occupation in which a solitary visitor, with one guide who knows everything, explores durable places and people who will not dismay him by altering. With those with whom he establishes a true relationship, it will be either that of a visitor penetrating for the first time into a new scene or personality, or that of a member of those caravans that revisited, with varying regularity, the oases of the desert. Not one of the friends he chooses will reject his friendship; not once will he leave with the foreboding that he will probably never be able to come back. The streets of Dublin on the 4th of May, the hawthorns of Combray, the Ugly Duchess's rose garden, are available.

As time goes on, he may even find, a little alarmingly, that certain companions of these fictive scenes are realer to him, form a more constant part of his consciousness, than some of his daily-life encounters. That is the time for a reminder that those denizens, those companions of wakeful nights, were once, somewhere, part of the flesh-and-blood world of their creators; in fact, that one of the breathless tourists now gaining the gangplank as the band strikes up "Mary Ann" may some day rest between the covers of a book, patiently waiting his arrival.

But will those covers be there? Will this particular form of travel become first a memory and then a fable?

Friends who are experts in such things tell me that for most of us the luxury of opening a book for selfish cause may become a luxury indeed. Crammed, bursting, erecting new buildings whose space is totally allocated before their walls are raised, libraries have their own population explosion. Microfilm will rescue us. But, like many other rescues, it will not be an altogether gentle salvation. It is the Mad Hatter's tea party all over again: No room! No room!

Obviously, we should be grateful for any sort of solution on the horizon; piles of books lie on the floor of the deepest stacks in huge libraries. And by some curious law, as fewer people seem to read books, more people seem to write them. It is, of course, good to know that the future traveler in those golden realms can plunge through a tiny entrance, into the scene he cares to visit. But there is always something a little solemn in a decline. Hundreds of children go to special museums to look, with lively speculation, at a train; if they can't be carried away by its wheels, they can view them, motionless. Blessed by that physical object, a book, it is natural to feel a fearful pang when faced with even the most fortunate device of substitution.

Well, we can only hope that our descendants, in their most nostalgic mood, will remember that a traveler, an ancestor, used to hold in her hand a book, and turn its pages.

The Handless Clock

I dropped my travel clock on cement; it bounced up with a curious result. It lost its hands, which slipped to the bottom of the crystal and crossed there. Otherwise, it was unaffected; it ticked briskly. I could wind it; had it had hands attached to its busy works, I could have set them. At first it seemed to me eerie, like a wingless bird. But it ticked, so I wound it; because I wound it, it ticked. We kept that up for some time.

Just then, I was working on poems about time and, in fact, a story, too. And that handless clock brought something into focus. It ticked off the minutes, all right; that precise number of seconds was slipping by, slipping by. It could tell me accurately that time was passing, but it could not tell me where I was in relation to that time. With a poet's devious instinct I understood that this was the exact metaphor for what I knew: that in a very real sense there is no true measurement for time in relation to the human being. Everyone feels some giant disparity between the hour mislaid in a great exhilaration and the hour lived through in waiting—for example, outside a hospital's surgical unit. Everyone feels it because it is real. The two times are quite different in length, in weight, even though the handless clock ticks away without pause.

It is easiest to sense this in direct confrontation with two extremes—the sense of exhaustion that flattens one after a day of split-second timing and the sense of the marvelous pause when the ticking seems to have dropped out of existence; even the memory of such pauses quickens the air. A treeful of lions, hanging like gross golden fruit from the thick branches of an

---

From *Baltimore Sun,* 20 January 1978.

African tree—heads propped in the crotch of a branch, furry pelts flacid along the limb, legs, tails, hanging limp and motionless. Not a stir of wind. Not a sound. Not an eye blink.

Very old places, too. The timeless feeling at high Lindos, where the time-defying columns stand up under the sky of Rhodes, and the anemones run like brushfire through the grass, and the rocks are warm to touch. Sometimes we are abashed to see how natural small disarrangements of time can be.

We went back to Lindos on a small bus, wanting to be there apart from a group, and as early in the morning as possible. We were the only Americans on the bus. It had a large swarthy handsome driver, who spoke a few words of English. A very old man, with a black knobby cane and a red handkerchief tucked round his neck, spoke a little, too—slowly, distinctly, with a pause between each word as though he were teaching us a language. The bus was full, mostly with women, their heads tied in scarves. When we got on, the old man spoke to us. "A fine morning," he said.

There were a great many stones in the road and a great many butterflies in the air. With the stopping and starting at tiny villages, we began to wonder tensely if we would ever get to the point of starting our climb.

Then in the center of nowhere, with a lurch, the bus stopped. We looked crossly around. Growing larger across the distance of a big field, slowly, slowly, a woman was walking toward the bus, steadily but quietly. On her left arm she carried a baby, her right propping its back. On she came, while the butterflies maneuvered their air levels and the bus shook rhythmically. We wondered wildly if anyone could just walk across a field from far away and halt the bus.

People stared through their windows but with no sign of impatience. The window by the bus driver was open, and he leaned slightly out with an expression of expectancy. Here, finally, came the woman. She was large, and she wore a large smile. Up to the bus she came but on the driver's side. Through the open window she handed him the baby. It was a fat, rather red-faced baby, and the driver received it with a burst of Greek. He set it on the wheel of the bus, where it sat, turning its head in wonder and stretching its fingers. The driver jumped it up and down, conversing with animation. The passengers watched, with a murmur of comment. Then the driver swung round, holding the baby higher. Pointing to his own chest, "Godson!" he said to the Americans.

The old man with the knobby cane leaned forward. "A boy," he said carefully. He set upon the words the approval he had set upon the day. "A fine boy," he repeated. We were unsure of the denouement had it been a wizened girl. There was a general murmur of acquiescence and pleasure. The driver held the baby high over his head again, brought it down and stuck it through the window, where the mother received it into its former position. The driver threw in the clutch, we surged forward, and a number of the passengers waved, to the baby, or the woman, or both. Looking back, we saw the woman standing looking after the bus. Then she turned and started steadily back across the field.

"A boy. A fine boy," said the old man, nodding to us, as we jolted forward to where Lindos would be right there, waiting.

Why You Not Say Good Morning?

A friend assures me that good manners can be—must be—regarded either as the art of fiction or as a disciplined system of lying. Either it is make-believe, for one's own pleasure and that of others, or it is the basis of a self-protective hypocrisy for getting through without giving or taking bruises, goes this theory. It could be interestingly defended.

What I long for, instead, is a fascinating treatise on the murky relationship between politeness and courtesy, which, in their striking resemblance, seem like siblings but, like siblings, often harbor a profound uncongeniality.

Notoriously, lack of space and time has radical effect on the behavior of animals that are the subjects of controlled experiments: the less of either time or space, the more irascibility, aggressiveness; resemblance to the nerves of five o'clock urban traffic. The absence of that involuntary act of the imagination which is courtesy is not the culprit of the evening melee. It is manners that were created, by cunning forebears lost in the mists of the past, to help. Hypocritical, invaluable, disciplined technique for handling the animal fury in the frustrated homeward-bound breast.

Children, fitted into manners with much bulging, cramping, and general distress—not to mention some loss of innocence—as into an all-purpose life jacket before a marine storm, seem to give a perfect example of the basic gap between manners and courtesy, that generously creative leap of identification. A fine courtesy comes naturally to a child. "That's *beautiful!*" they tell you seriously of your misshapen drawing. Baking mudpies,

From *Baltimore Sun*, 22 June 1979.

"Don't you want one?" they anxiously ask. But, once abandoned of that involuntary sense of identification: "Who let *him* in?" they wonder aloud, of the unfamiliar guest; "What makes her *nose* so funny?" they ask with a limpid scientific interest. Failing to identify with a contemporary in possession of a toy truck, they simply hit him over the head with what comes to hand.

Manners will fix all that, but what a tricky tool they are. Unlike courtesy—international, interracial, internal—they differ wildly, discrete as a language. Is greeting a stranger polite or intrusive? Is cordiality called for, or will it be seen as ingratiation? Will the omission of a local system of formality mark you as a boor? In her "Autobiography" Agatha Christie points out that, while in Turkey she discovered that to beckon means "Please go away," to push the hand against the air in a gesture of dismissal means "Please, come here."

On a small island four of us were lost, already late for lunch on a cocoa plantation. Potholed roads branched in every direction through vistas of mangoes, sapodilla trees, giant vines, and house-high ferns. At a little crossroads, in the shade, three men sat on a fence. We pulled in front of them, and their conversation stopped.

"Can you tell us how to get to the Brent plantation?" one of us cried.

There was a pause, while the car ticked in the heat and a dog barked somewhere. Then the man in the middle looked at us, not with hostility but severely.

"Why you not say, 'Good morning!?' " he asked.

An instant, while we all looked at one another; then, partly irritated, partly sheepish, "Good morning!" we chorused.

"Good morning!" said the man in the middle, and "Good morning!" said the men on either side. Our rebuker left the fence and came over to the car, raising a long black finger. "You go so," he said, and gave us complex and correct directions. We lurched forward, calling back "Thank you! Goodbye!"

We attempted to imagine, on a four-lane highway—cars palpitating at a red light—tooting our horn; and, as a harassed face leaned from another screwed-down window and the light changed, calling "Good morning!" the last word lost in the cataclysm of horns. But, on the island, none of us again asked a question unpreceded by a formal greeting. Courtesy's imagination having failed us, local manners took charge.

There is a lively business being done by the intimidation-through-insult school, now pulling in shekels from a dozen printing presses. Earnest practitioners, preaching over their shoulders en route to their caring bank, explain to us the power of the put-down, the exhilarating freedom of mutual insult, the effect on boss or headwaiter of thinly veiled contempt. Fascinatingly, as these pioneers multiply, a gelatinous response is raised, which plays straight into their capable hands. It ignores the fact that "your friendly grocer," "you nice people, you deserve everything we do for you" (quite possibly true), translates itself perversely as "Drop dead, Bud."

Insult, or buttering up, aside, there is a daring doctrine that offers to negotiate free of manners, as a confident aerialist may decide to abandon a net. It is we, unfortunately, who plunge.

Perhaps we must put manners, as such, in the category of the whooping crane, nearly extinct wildflowers, and certain ancient and persistent species of fish.

Openness, a Vast Confusion

Accessibility has become a curious thing. How easy is it to get in? To stay out? Small physical possessions have developed unexpected resources of resistance: a carton of half-and-half; a turn-cap soft drink; a can of smoked oysters; medicine, clearly visible in resolutely sealed vials. Pull where the finger points; the carton refuses to part its lips; rip desperately, and a three-pronged jet of creamy milk or milky cream dots the dress and floor. The fluted metal cap will not turn. The key to the oyster can snaps, and the can's rounded corners reject it rhythmically from the can opener. The midnight headache must be stiff-upper-lipped, short of rousing the household. Lips with arrow: press down while turning. By not one pacifying pellet shall the contents be reduced tonight.

The only burst of genuine human sympathy for the wakeful figure in the White House I remember experiencing during all of Watergate's interminability was when I read of the tooth marks on the lid of the sedative plastic vial. Mon semblable, mon frere!

And, yet, how accessible other things have become—as accessible as a missing stairtread or an open grating. It may be a battle for access to one's cream or one's aspirin, but instant help is sucking at one's feet like the hose of a vacuum. Dowdy? Frigid? Tasteless? Shunned? For as much as a few thousand, for as little as a quarter, rescue is here; above all, is instant. At the top, by expensive arrangement; at the bottom, close as the supermarket's checkout rack.

Are *you* Open? is the question. Do you wish to join in giving

---

From *Baltimore Sun,* 15 March 1979.

the Primal Scream to relieve tensions? Do you wish a toe-to-toe confrontation in which the effect of your instant personality will be verbalized? How accessible are you? Is your first name as available as the nickel? Jim, this is Lucy; Jody, this is Sam. Do you malinger, in the parachute drop into intimacy? Ah, you are not open. It is to no avail that what is really not open is your half-and-half.

Let there be no shadow of criticism for those for whom this works. May their homes, their spouses, their acceptability, thrive and blossom. Yet there persists the residue of those for whom it is the can, the capsule, and the carton that should be instantly accessible.

In a fit of despondency, in which I began to wonder if the desire to confer one's first name as a token of a friendship ripening like a peach, represented a neurosis, I recently became involved in a conversation with a middle-aged Frenchman. I was asking, a little timidly, about the nuances of salutation between French ladies of normal accessibility. It proved more intricate than I had bargained for. Well: two ladies thrown often together (but basically strangers) for an indefinite period greet each other pleasantly, one lady saying, "Bonjour, Madame," to which the second will respond, "Bonjour, Madame." Eventually, informed by an unexpressed but active sense of cordiality, the first lady will burst forth, "Bonjour, Madame Piquot," to which the second, warming, will respond, "Bonjour, Madame Verlaine." A totally new relationship. And, as a final sealing of congeniality, later, "Bonjour, Jacqueline!" "Ah, bonjour Madeleine." This, I must say, seemed a trifle formal, and I said so. He looked at me for a moment. Then, "But Madame," he said, "it is, you see, an affair of *gradations,*" and suddenly I was home free. This was not my tempo, but this was my touchstone. Gradations. The stages by which acquaintance becomes congeniality, congeniality becomes intimacy. Everyone has experienced a lightning flash of intimacy—with a child, with a stranger. But it is not accidental or casual; it is the flowering of long preparation.

As it becomes more and more difficult to control the accessibility of one's possessions, it becomes more and more difficult to resist accessibility to that section of one's life that one has the right to control . . . one's predilections, vagaries, joys, and companionships.

There seems to be some vast confusion between friendliness and intimacy. (In optimistic moments we think of the former as especially and characteristically American—surely, one of our most endearing offerings.) The latter, tricky, special, the final flower of a process. Every child who has tried to pry loose the gripped petals of a bud to see at once the loose, unfolded secret of the full bloom knows how hopeless is the forced instant blossom. That loosening has been prepared by earth and roots and weather, rain and sun, heat and chill.

But it is very scary to lie under the imputation of a lack of openness. Truly, to have been given an open nature is the first of the godmother's gifts. But open to what? The magazine decorator, the best-seller sex manual, the look-out-for-number-one paranoia? It is, as my admonishing Gallic friend remarked, indeed an affair of gradations.

Align arrow, press down while turning. No need of ripening there. What is needed there is Openness—instant intimacy.

Breaking Bread Together

Breaking bread together has always and everywhere been associated with peace and friendship. The acquiring of clothing has never been an especially communal occasion. Sex is more or less private. Barn raisings and housewarmings are special events, out of the tide of daily custom. But the sharing of nourishment is an immediate theme in myth and tribal history.

George Barnard Shaw was horrified that people should gather together to indulge in something as unalluring as he felt eating to be. On being invited to lunch by an old friend, he telegraphed that he would be unable to attend, "in view of my well-known habits"—to which his would-be hostess spiritedly telegraphed back: "Know nothing of your habits. Hope they are not so bad as your manners."

Bread and wine maintain their ancient aura of hospitality, through all the varied, less and more fortunate forms of food and drink. An Englishman happily told me—he having just emerged from one—that the American cocktail party was the only place in the world where one could shout to one's vis-à-vis, "I'm *so* glad your dog died!" and have the vis-à-vis shout back, "Isn't it!" At such parties there is always a deserted or saturnine solitary, sitting or standing, visible in the corner of the host's eye. Shall she (he) be ignored or a rescue operation launched? Years ago, one guest, sent on such a mission, approached Miss Dorothy Parker, glowering on the outskirts. "And what are *you* having?" he hospitably demanded. "Not much fun," said Miss Parker.

The food and drink of the cocktail party have slid quite a way

---

From *Baltimore Sun,* 12 February 1980.

from their ancient concerns: other problems emerge. Why did every guest decide, as though in consultation, to drink only gin, thus causing it to run out? Who could have anticipated the mutual hostility between smoker and nonsmoker? (Well, in retrospect, almost anyone.) How could the pitcher of auxiliary martinis have been mistaken for water for the bourbon?

In the days when I still planned to visit all the countries of the earth, I was discouraged by the prospect of confrontation with strange foods. One of my concerns was sheeps' eyes. Would I be able graciously to consume those snared for me by my Arab host plunging his arm into the bowl, under the desert skies? It turned out that these, like so many worries, were irrelevant; it was not sheeps' eyes that thwarted my ambition.

Yet, with all the remote or debased or boring variations—the noisy, the disorderly, the indifferent, the heavily public—there remains something ancient and durable, and sustaining in more than the physical sense, in sitting down, in peace with friends to break bread.

Not all memorable meals celebrate food or friendship. I remember a dinner at a seedy Barbadian guest house, where we had finally landed, repenting at leisure our habit of letting the future, and reservations, take care of themselves. We sat at a long table, crowded by tourists of three nationalities, many of them house residents. The solitary waiter, who minutes earlier had been the solitary barman, was very drunk, perhaps in despair at the enormity of his task. His bow tie rested like a butterfly below his left ear, and his gaze was remote. He attempted a number of times to pass a dish of callaloo to a loud bald tourist in full cry, who ignored him. Finally, solemnly raising his two middle fingers, he knocked sharply on the exact center of the guest's bald head, obtaining his result. I have always remembered him fondly.

One might say that, in the original garden, the sharing of food got off to a shaky start. But somehow, through all ages and all cultures, the breaking of bread together has been a central motif and its subversion by any sort of treachery the darkest betrayal. Infamous cases of this stand out in history. A horrifying instance occurred not many years ago, when members of a primitive tribe, accepting the hospitality of a feast, were subsequently slaughtered. In simple societies hospitality was so sacred a matter that it often came before the interests of the household and of the host himself. Since the dimmest reaches of time, people have gathered together under this sign of amity, so that grain and grape have been more than themselves. Can hospitality, in this immemorial sense, survive all its unprepossessing kith and kin—the quick counter lunch, the high-pressure business meal, the TV dinner? The answer is that it seems to be one of the few things truly indestructible.

International Aspects of the Mad Hatter

I am, most honestly, an Anglophile—by part origins, by Shakespeare, by tea, by "Wind in the Willows"; most of all, by friends. My problem, and it is one that I find many of my English friends appreciate fully, is that of a traditional misunderstanding, a myth on which we have been nourished: that the English are the bud and blossom of Lord Chesterfield's dictum that a gentleman is one who is never unintentionally rude. If there is truth in that dictum drunk in with one's mother's milk, then there must exist Englishmen and women who are in trouble. Deep trouble.

This was originally borne in on me when a truly charming Englishman, then functioning in the diplomatic service (square peg in a round hole?), on coming to dinner, fervently congratulated me, as his hostess, on our home. "But it's charming!" he cried. "Such pri–vacy!" as he looked at our oaks and arborvitae. "You would never think you were in an American home!"

And so it has gone. For years the English have complimented me on my manner of speech: "One would never think you were an American!" I almost gave an endearing Englishman, sharing planter's punches with me in a tropical clime, a heart attack from delighted shock one evening. He had been discoursing on Hyde Park, and we had reached the paths along the Serpentine. I offered an automatic, "Ah, Peter Pan . . . ." His drink almost shot from his hand. "My *dear!*" he shouted to his wife, deep in converse with my husband. They turned startled faces. Wildly, my transatlantic cousin indicated me. "She knows about Peter

---

From *Baltimore Sun,* 7 April 1979.

Pan!" It would be almost redundant to recount an almost identical colloquy aboard an ocean liner, on the score of the Mad Hatter. "The Mad *Hatter!* She knows . . . ."

In a lovely suburb near London, our Virginia hostess, encountering a British neighbor, as in an icy July drizzle we all gravitated homeward down the lane, yearned toward him in the engaging if suspect humility of a Virginia hostess. "Last time you came for dinner," she lamented, "we gave you a dreadful meal. Next time, you'll see, we'll do better!"

The object of this reassurance made a series of complex sounds in his throat. "Um, ah," he said. "Yes, well, I'll remember that." We walked along, hunched soddenly in our coats. "Keith will be going to the States next month," said our hostess brightly, undaunted. "*How* I dread the New York weather," said Keith, the neighbor. "Last time it nearly killed me," he added strongly.

At a recent professional gathering, divided roughly between Americans and their transatlantic cousins, the Americans spoke to the visitors of lawns (English), roses (English), Dickens (English). Our visitors spoke of children (American), steam heat (American), and Dickens—specifically, of his masterpiece *Martin Chuzzlewit* and, more specifically, of its masterpiece-within-a-masterpiece, his American travels. Openly, or secretly, all of the natives blushed, remembering the tobacco juice sprayed at poor Mr. Dickens in all areas of the country. That evening I sat next to a witty and amiable Englishman doomed to watch on TV one of the final games of the World Series. It was obvious that, if, after years, cricket remains a mystery to me, the esoteric goings-on on the screen had him paralyzed. After a particularly grueling inning, he turned to commiserate with me. "Isn't it a shame they chew so much gum?" he said. Since we seemed headed back for *Martin Chuzzlewit* by one route or another, I chose the shortest. Accurately or not, "That's not gum," I said. "That's tobacco." "Oh," he said. "Ah yes. Yes, of course," he added hastily.

Among detective story authors my favorites all are British. They write with urbanity, trenchancy, and realistic detail. By experience, or research, they are accurate about the most arcane primitive rites in remote areas or the nuances of medical developments or the temperamental variations in the French

Sureté. Then, on shipboard or in an astounded drawing room, appear an American couple. "Well, Mother," says the American gentleman to his wife, "I guess that was a real genteel lady, all right, we were chewing the fat with yesterday."

"You can say that again, Father," she responds.

"I'll say you're cooking with gas!" cries the American professor in agreement.

That evening, "Well, I reckon you sure are a great little looker!" shouts the millionaire from the States, as he is introduced to his host's daughter.

Ah well. Root affection stands firm. Yet sometimes, in the self-indulgence of daydreams, I compose a letter to a mythical British friend, whose distinguished brother has just completed a visit to our shores. The letter varies; it varies greatly. But sometimes it goes something like this.

> Dearest Jill:
>
> I can't tell you how we've enjoyed Derek. He was absolutely marvelous, and we all adored him. Nobody would believe that he was English! Do you know, Jill, he got the point of every single story. He never dropped one single aitch the entire time he was here. And Jill—Jill, he knew that Moby-*Dick* was a *whale!*

Mayed and Traught on a Desert Island

Everyone has been subjected to someone else's choice of reading matter on a desert island. But oddly, among the throng of dispersing Crusoes armed with a Bible or the *Collected Works of William Shakespeare,* a most obvious choice seems to be scanted. Does no one long for an Unabridged Dictionary? True, it could not be carried comfortably about—it would have to serve as a sort of shrine to which the marooned solitary could come to while away the long hot hours when there is no sound but the soft smash of waves and the light clatter of wind in the palms.

Here is a wealth so deep that a shipwrecked lifetime could scarcely exhaust it. After the empty horizon is scanned again and sandy fingers lift the cover, what is promised? Anatomy, Anthropology, Applied Science; Architecture, Arts, Astronomy; Botany, Building Trades; Chemistry, Coins, Commerce—and we have reached only our ABCs.

By the time our solitary has come through to Weights and Measures, Wines, Spirits, and Beer, and finally reached Zoology, it is apparent that his problem will be a precipitate sail, before he has accomplished his treasures. Say that he estimates a pre-rescue period of twenty-six months: he will have to absorb one formal letter, as, *A,* in a month, thirty-one quick days, or an even more hurried thirty.

There will be an exotic: "Aardwolf—A striped hyena-like African mammal." The confusing: "All fours—All of four legs of an animal, or both arms and legs of man." (Or woman?)

From *Baltimore Sun,* 18 July 1980.

The terse: "All in—Exhausted." The comfortable: "Alpaca—A domesticated, sheeplike ruminant, having long silky hair or wool." Horticultural-poetic: "Amaranth—*Poetic,* a flower that never fades. Of the genus Amaranthus, which includes love-lies-bleeding." The possibly present?: "Ambergris—A morbid secretion of the sperm whale, fragrant when heated, usually found floating on the ocean or cast ashore." Terrifying: "Amoeba—A microscopic one-celled animal consisting of a naked mass of protoplasm constantly changing in shape as it moves and engulfs food."

Royal Annes, he finds, are known exclusively as appendages of their husbands: "Anne of Austria: Queen of Louis XIII." "Anne of Bohemia: Queen of Richard II." "Anne of Cleves: Fourth wife of Henry VIII."

There are fascinating juxtapositions: "Apollo—1. Greek (and Roman) deity, the god of light, healing, music, poetry, prophecy. 2. A very beautiful young man," is neighbored by "Apollyon—The destroyer. Angel of the bottomless pit."

Then, though he cannot use it at the moment, the wonderful "Avast—Stop! hold! cease! stay!"

While he moves steadily through fields of strange knowledge, he may pause, lifting his eyes to the blue and green above, and the surrounding sea, to wonder what has happened to the words whose negative sense alone remains: *un,* and *in,* and *dis.* Dismayed. What ever happened to *mayed?* Or *traught?* Or *tracted?* They must all have been happy states.

Though *in* has prevailed, what about *ane* and *ept?* He will hear Bert Lahr's angry protest, "I am as ept as anybody! Maybe epter!"

Un has brought things from bad to worse. Where are the "nerved," the "manned"?

Why is it always the good, the happy state, that has disappeared? Perhaps, in a Whitmanesque revolt, he can compose a song-of-himself:

> Away with your in, your dis.
> I defy your un.
> I ept, I ert, I ane.
> Beach, sea, I address you,

I mayed, I traught, I gruntled,
etc. etc. etc.

But to get back to his progress. The crowded days tick by. In the midst of his *Zs*, on the horizon a sail appears, unobserved. "Zany" he reads, "An apish person or clown." "Zephyr—A soft, mild breeze. *Poetic,* the west wind personified." "Ziggurat—A temple of Sumerian origin in the form of a pyramidal tower."

He lifts his eyes, envisioning terraced slopes, and there, distinctly, is an oncoming sail.

No matter how feverishly he reads, he will never have it all. "Zingara—A female gypsy." "Zipangu—Marco Polo's name for Japan." "Zombi—1. The python god among certain W. Africans. 2. The snake god worshiped in the voodoo ceremonies of the West Indies."

Now he can make out tiny figures at the deckrail. "Zucchetto—A small round skull-cap worn by Roman Catholic ecclesiastics, a priest's being black, a bishop's, violet, a cardinal's, red, the Pope's, white."

But it is no use.

A keel grates on the sand. He struggles to lift his Unabridged, to stagger with it into the vines and creepers. Too late.

"Zwieback—(twice baked) A kind of bread cut into . . " is his last glimpse.

His final glimpse. There will be dictionaries at home. But will he have time to read them? Un-heard of.

To Our Waiting Names

Someone must write a book about names, just names. Proust had dozens of pages on place names; Eudora Welty has a fine essay on this. But this entire book would be about that fascinating and basically mysterious subject.

It would have a chapter on the enormous weight of a name. The beasts Adam named have carried that identity ever since. Somehow humans feel that the name is the first, the essential knowledge. A five-year-old, confronted by a new contemporary, takes a good long stare and then says, "What's your name?" And in some primitive tribes the name was so precious, so loaded with magic, that knowledge of it gave the possessor power over its owner. So he had his real, his secret, name, known only to himself and to his gods, and then the utilitarian name by which he was known to others.

This would lead to a chapter on the helplessness with which we bear the label we never chose. There are groups that often do something about that: actors, writers, and the owners of those immobile full-face-and-profiles that gaze at, and away from, us in every rural post office. Often these last have a series of choices: aka . . . . But most of us never meddle with something that has become a part of ourselves before we think of it. Until very recently most women slipped easily from their own surname to another, belonging to a man, keeping only the Mary or Helen conferred by their parents as unshakable identification. Now many keep "their" name. But unless they go all the way to *X*, they are still carrying the name of a man that has absorbed that of a woman. The Spanish made a stab at a more imaginative

From *Baltimore Sun,* 25 January 1979.

approach, but who is going through American life as Amy Jones y Murphy?

And then there will be a chapter on the sound of names that ring like authentic coins down through the ages. Thermopylae, Salamis; Tutankhamen; Tamburlaine. Certain names in themselves send out a sort of nimbus of drama. When Tamburlaine cries out,

> Is it not brave to be a king, Techneles,
> And ride in triumph through Persepolis?

it is the names that echo. And where could le Grand Charles possibly have had a home except in Colombey-les-Deux-Eglises? And this would lead to a chapter about the accumulated burden on the bearers of famous names . . . the actor, whose performance is always compared to some previous highspot; the politician, impaled on a statement made under his name a dozen years ago; the writer, hag ridden by expectations of his admirers who want him to continue doing what no longer interests him. In a small book Matisse wrote on jazz, he comments on the practice of the Japanese artists of an earlier era who, at some middle point in life, laboring under their reputations, accomplishments, and projects, simply changed their identities, starting quite freshly with a new name, blank as a page.

Then comes a chapter on the echoes left by names . . . those of the native, the conqueror, the colonists, who have lapsed into history, leaving as traces the French names, the Indian names, the Spanish names, that we pronounce without thought. In New England the beautiful hushing sound of Indian names is everywhere: Massachusetts, Ammanousic, Winnipesaukee. The French names of northern New Hampshire: Bigaud, Drouin, Gautier; the Spanish names of the West: Los Angeles, Santa Fe, San Diego. A confused and earnest friend, preparing my mother for her trip to La Jolla, told her, "Now remember: it's *spelled L A J O L L A*, but it's *pronounced* Tijuana."

And certainly a chapter on the nostalgia of small American villages (with a main street, two gas stations, and a cat asleep in a grocery store window) named Venice or Florence, Crete, or Rome, Athens, Paris. Had whoever named them seen the mother city or island? Did they hope to go? All over the country, in every state, they dot the map, with their invisible gondolas, piazzi, and tavernas.

And an ominous chapter about names and numbers. Names, more and more, trail numbers behind them, attached by multiplying threads; your name, yes, but your Social Security number, your Blue Cross number, your phone, credit card, street, zip number. In prisons the number is in possession. But it encroaches—perhaps the chapter should end in the shock of the future in which names have altogether disappeared or will be an intimate vagary, used as a code word among friends.

A brisk matron told me not long ago that she had no patience with this nonsense about an identity crisis. "I," she said, "have always known exactly who I am." Always? Exactly?

Perhaps the last chapter will end with that first moment of consciousness, when the eyes open to morning light, and in that infinitesimal instant before time and place mesh, in a strange free float, we reach out from the dark of sleep to our waiting names.

Artifacts of Memory

Archaeology, the dictionary says, is "the study of material remains of past human life and activities." More than that, it is the seedbed of memory, and its fascination comes from the leap we take into continuity.

Trudging the sun-baked streets of Pompeii, bombarded by the guide's dramatic inaccuracies, what we really look at, look for, are resemblances with familiar things: this atrium where guests gathered, noisily conversational; that room where hungry and thirsty people ate fruit and drank wine. We know that when the hot ashes fell people were selling and buying; taking a nap; bathing; worrying; arranging flowers; making love.

The knowledge is partly a tiny chill, partly a warmth of recognition. It is like a hand touching our shoulder. What we are really concerned with is not the dead but the living: those people, then; us, now.

Theirs was a sophisticated generation, concerned with many of the things that concern us. But going back into time, our archaeologist brings up to the sun traces of an age buried profoundly in the past. It is, as a book title tersely put it, *The Testimony of the Spade.* And again we feel, this time more strangely, the combined chill and warmth: this woman prepared food for her children; that man built a fire for protection and warmth; and when night fell they wanted fire and shelter and human company.

Art was imitation and magic—but something else, too. In the caves of Lascaux the innermost and highest paintings were too high to have been visible by any illumination then possessed; the

---

From *Baltimore Sun,* 24 September 1980.

artist was not painting for the observer. In the dizzying tables of centuries how very close they are to us, the vanguard of a beleagured and recent army of human beings.

Archaeology has a way of slipping out of its technical boundaries—it haunts all aspects of memory. Planting a garden, on an early June morning, a rubber soldier is unearthed; and that tiny object, grubby, one-legged, recreates instantly a June a quarter of a century gone by, the heat, the flowers, the voice, the gesture. Was the rubber man buried by accident or with ceremony? Like any vessel or trinket or tool, it speaks of its owner, demands our recognition.

It is the same with a blackened chimney, strangled by wild roses, with no house to warm. We are stopped suddenly by the hieroglyph, which will tell us nothing except that someone passed here and paused, for years or decades, a message we will never translate more accurately but cannot fail to understand.

The fascination of ghost stories is the fascination of archaeology. Ghosts are revenants; they *revisit* the glimpses of the moon. Who were you? we ask. Did you live here? What happened to you? What do you want? There are, so to speak, implicit as well as explicit ghosts. Standing in the great square of Monte Alban in quiet sunlight, the visitor finds it enigmatically peopled, crowded with its own life, priests, warriors, victims. The ball court, where to lose the game was to lose life, vibrates with its players.

Psychiatrists are archaeologists. Who are you? they ask. What happened to you? Let us excavate that minute, that incident, that morning twenty years ago, that childhood night.

We are ourselves archaeologists. Come back in early May to a house shut up through a mountain winter. The time-lapse is not centuries but months. Yet it is the past we explore as surely as though it were six centuries. It is, indeed, the past. In the wastebasket is the stub of a ticket for the barn theater, whose actors, like their audience of that summer night, are elsewhere. The calendar on the kitchen wall is for an October gone with its leaves. In the porch rafters a sluttish bunch of twigs held eggs, now wings, and on the big lilac bush by the door brown lumps are the traces of purple cones that drew hordes of Monarch butterflies, come three thousand miles from a Mexico winter, to wave and fan in the heat. In the attic playroom burly logs are ashes in the chunk stove; a broken crayon drew something unpreserved. It is a rare house that will have no trace of someone who will not come back.

Making us human, layer on layer the artifacts of memory lie. The pharaohs, all the emperors who designed tombs of magnificence, simply say together: Remember me. Layer on layer, the cities lie. In the mind, layer on layer of memory. In the house, summer on summer, its hours and minutes. From the men of Lascaux to last year's June, the distance is short.

Time Out of Mind

There were always fairy stories in which, when the humans went to bed, the toys came to life—like all fairy tales, these were a little frightening.

There is an ambiguity in shapes. What we are familiar with suddenly shows us the oddest face. Like the images in a Rorschach blot, the tame and accustomed shapes in a nursery grow strange, even ominous, in the semidark. The corner of a bureau is a horse's head, turned attentively toward the bed; the dark cushion tossed on a chair develops ears and a jaw. The nightlight has either conjured the unreal or revealed a secret.

Our security blanket of custom comforts us from too sharp a sight or ear. Who would have believed, before the transistor, that our silent room was a babble of speech, music, other voices and other languages? Now we have been forcibly made aware of the activity of our very houseplants: their disguised motion, their receptivity to our tones of voice, our identity. Is nothing faithfully familiar?

We know this strangeness is true of rooms—preeminently of mirrors. Who hasn't suddenly walked into an empty room and been conscious of something just vanished into the mirror's depths; of furniture just immobilized, the chairs holding out their arms, like players in the game of Steps when It opens its eye? But this is true, too, of places.

I have seen a house's surrounding landscape, balanced on the delicate edge of country and suburbia, protect itself in this way. It sits at the edge of a driveway of thick pines, directly off the quintessence of suburbia. Opposite the driveway of pines,

---

From *Baltimore Sun,* 19 December 1979.

the rich billiard table green of a golf course undulates. There is a bricky flash of fine tennis courts, and huge rubber dolphins fraternize chastely in the swimming pool. Geranium, delphinium, and petunia are pleasantly exploited.

The driveway through the rackety pines leads to the back of a house, wooden, Victorian, not recently painted. Its front is away from the driveway; it faces a rough lawn, then a field, the woods, the mountains. From the shaggy grass beyond its porch no human habitation is visible.

At each end of the porch, which faces the woods, a great granite slab appears. All day the screen door bangs; lawnmowers, tires, distant voices sound. Birds fly around, but they are decorative, like the flowers.

After dark the noises diminish. Out front, very late, there are no lights anywhere, except in the sky. Far beyond the driveway pines, down the road, the hotel still blazes; tires sing at longer intervals. After midnight reality surfaces.

The granite is glacier old. The ferns that grow around it have not altered their ancient forms. The moon comes up. Sap moves in the trees. In the meadow grass, innumerable lives begin, end, continue. Sometimes there is a small shriek: an owl is hunting or even, sometimes, a fox. The changeless sound of leaves sifted by the wind is there. The house rests on its granite like a bubble. It is then that the mountains emerge from the tiny covering of hours. Like giants that all day pretend to be the inanimate playground of children, openly they resume their lives.

To catch a glimpse of it happening is like a sharp quick immersion into the element of strangeness, of the ancient. The boulder rejoins its family, stone everywhere, in all the unimagined stone of the earth. The mountains, which shift and move in their own time, not ours, are part of mountains under seas, mountains lost and rising. And the earth itself, giving and taking, resumes its relations with time-out-of-mind.

It happens late every night—but so unobtrusively as to seem secretive.

If a human comes out onto the porch at dawn, everything has withdrawn into heavy, preparatory mist; there is a particular soundlessness. Then as a sort of sentinel, a changing of the guard, a bird calls, and dimly the appropriate objects of the day begin to appear: the rocks of the wall, points of the wood's spruces, a dew-frosted patch of lawn.

Now it all begins again. The trimmers of lawns, the rollers of greens, the sprayers of courts, are up and about. The isolation facing the porch has changed; it is bland, a perquisite.

It is probably a good thing that it happens mostly, so to speak, behind the back. It is pleasant to decorate the earth with petunias, to form a birdbath from a basin in the boulder, to have a mountain view. It is good to cut the hair of the earth, and decorate stone with dwarf iris, and hang a chart that names the peaks. It is pleasant that the owners look out from the porch at what is theirs, and familiar.

At certain hours.

A Generous Disorder

The war lasted all summer. There were sallies and provocations to which we paid no attention or, at most, a resigned acknowledgment. The small dark mole, in his world of roots, grubs, and fibers, heaved up into the night air, on our already rackety lawn. The red squirrels, the fledglings' enemies, insinuated themselves miraculously between inner and outer wall and stamped about in the waste and middle of the night, with a scurrying clatter of claws, causing houseguests to start out of sleep or dream of doom and pursuit. Tiny mounds of mysterious sand blossomed on the grass, with a traffic hole, like a small dark eye, at the center: the city of the ants.

A rasping saw, night after night, rose from the spot at which some substructure of our aged house was being systematically, happily, gnawed. A porcupine. Prowling, we never saw him, except once by day, high in the tip of a tree, like a sailor in the crow's nest. A neighbor, who knows everything, advised us to distract the porcupine from his dismantling project, by pickling a steak and leaving it on the adjacent pine needles. Pickling a *steak?* For the *porcupine?* A stake, it turned out, pickled in brine. This was *suses fou* but resulted in a perfect convocation of porcupines: ecstatic shufflings, grunts, and gnawing. We gave it up, and, after a few nights in which the porcupines were indeed fretful, we were left with our original and indigenous wrecker.

But with the garden, détente dropped to nil. There was nothing, absolutely nothing, except the marigolds and—blessedly—the tomatoes that lacked its special gourmand.

The buds of the portulaca, we discovered, were the delicacies

---

From *Baltimore Sun,* 14 July 1978.

of the skunk family. A pair lived under our wing—in both senses of the word—raised three extremely pretty kits, and behaved irreproachably, except that the red, orange, magenta, and acid yellow buds, just on opening, were devoured totally. The brilliant black and white stripes, once caught feeding on that rainbow, were almost worth the disaster.

An immense rabbit, curdling our memories of *Watership Down,* leapt the fence to feast on all the green beans. The Mexican zinnias, forming tips of those basic clashing colors that Mexican sap miraculously harmonizes, were clipped to the earth as they pointed enough to hint their colors, by the groundhog. The slow, slow ripening of the corn inside its silk, and crispy husk, reached the perfect point for the quick sinewy racoon fingers (God knows how *he* got in . . .) just before attaining ripeness for human taste. Who would know that deer love lettuce? They must have sailed photogenically over the fence to plant those sharp, meticulous hoof marks down the row.

The blueberries, like the gourds of cocoa on tropical bushes, ripened in simultaneous stages; green, green stained with violet, purple, swelled out with a full misty bloom. The gardener covered the entire long row of bushes with a great drapery of white gauze, so that a vast Chinese caterpillar-dragon blazed in the sun and wanly shone by moonlight. Success. Angry cries, hovering wings, greed baffled by the superior brain. One day a sharp flapping under the gauze: a terrified bird. The terror lasted the seconds before his mates arrived. The whole snowy worm heaved and rocked within. Perhaps if the gardener had nailed it to the ground with a thousand spikes . . . ?

In the frosty autumn nights the bears visited the remoter apple trees. Spoor and claw marks on the trunks; a broken branch or two. Hibernation coming up.

The gardener's wife hungered for the supermarket; it appeared to her in dreams, majestic, ordered, the triumph of distant battles fought in her behalf.

Now, in a mean February dusk, that is where she is. The neon stare of the wide chilly aisles is over the long line of wicker pushcarts, metal to metal, curving from each checkout. Tinned or fresh, rank on rank, the earth's produce is around her. At the moment, she is trapped in the express lane. The lady presently checking out has not gotten her bananas weighed. Worse, the basket pusher directly ahead has thirteen distinctly and ascertainable items in the express line. They are not even decently concealed under one another. The queue's sacredness is violated; low growls run through the line, remarks sideslip from curled lips. Will the checkout lady repudiate the attempt? Will the subversive be sent to the rear of the longer line? Ah, here are the bananas now . . . . The thirteen items are cheerfully rung up.

Outside, in the snow sleet, a vast paved desert glitters with the unbroken metallic ranks of cars. To the right of the gardener's wife are piled slick, pale tomatoes, shiny in their juiceless heaps. To her left, at eye level, is the hateful rack of words, proclaiming this week's cure for cancer, sex problems, and carpet stains.

It is seasonal nostalgia, lacking all good sense—but at the moment upsurges the smell of night grasses heavy with dew and pine scent; the image of the riotous moonlit feast of the hungry and the agile; the clear, finicky print of the deer hoofs; the juice spurting from swollen blueberries clustered in their leaves' brilliance; the snapped twigs and harsh scoring of bear claws on loaded apple boughs; the generous disorder of daring.

The bananas, weighed, are gone; the thirteen items bagged. The gardener's wife is here for nourishment. The questions are where, how, and what.

Trees

A friend of mine, a man devoutly dedicated to trees, owns half a tree. The tree, a lavish oak, grows exactly on the line between his property and that of his Cambridge neighbors. His half provides shade for a beautiful yard banked with rhododendrons, high-fenced for privacy, and quite sylvan, considering its position on the corner of a busy street. Not unnaturally, the lavish oak also provides shade for a considerable area of the neighbor's property, on just the location where the neighbor's wife proposes a flowerbed. The neighbor sent word, politely ahead of time, that he would be having the oak "removed." This euphemism for destruction enraged my friend, the descendant of a long line of hamadryads. His succinct response was "Never."

Negotiations over drinks having abysmally failed, an impasse emerged reminiscent of that of King Solomon's baby case. The matter went to court.

And what did the court say? My friend becomes so emotional at this point that it is a bit hard to sort things out clearly. But what does develop without doubt is the decision that the tree must go. (Could this be prompted by the Puritan ethic that pleasure must yield to purpose, leisure in the shade to activity in the sun?) So, relations are frosty, my friend misanthropic, and the tree doomed. One can only hope, weakly, that the flowers will be magnificent. But, in comparison to the massive presence of an oak, delphinium? Gladioli?

I side with my friend, through more than friendship. It seems to me that, if we played a variation on the what-book-would-you-take-to-a-desert-island game and I were forced to choose one

---

From *Baltimore Sun,* 17 April 1980.

field of vision in which to take refuge from moments of urban crisis, it would be in the world of trees. A kind of implicit majesty has little to do with size; the giant sequoias, the mammoth tree of Tula, are overwhelming, but it is the tree nature itself that seems to shelter and somehow deeply reassure.

Trees were an important part of childhood. In books, they displayed the giant twisted roots among which the provident leprechaun disappeared, or the somber forest over which Kay flew with the Snow Queen. In leafy reality, they were privacy and magic. When I lived in the North, I spent hours in the crotch of a dogwood. Given both height and secrecy, I could cling quietly, close to the leveling branches of flat flawed flowers around me; in early autumn, if I sat still enough, birds gathered in a small uproar over the red berries. When I lived in the South, back I went into the trees like a marmoset; long-leaf pine with dry spicy tassels and drops of bright sticky sharp-smelling resin on the slick small boughs.

Now we have what we fondly call an orchard; it consists of five apple trees. In the cold New Hampshire May mornings, they put out the most defenseless-looking clusters of rose and white, against the cold glossy bark. And in September, hour after hour, they drop heavy red globes into the matted field grass with the faintest of thuds.

But, as with horses and dogs, there is something domestic about fruit trees. Even in their dazzling bloom or faint promise on a Van Gogh canvas, they are beautifully, dutifully, serving. But the oaks, the vanishing elms, the crowds of white birches in the mountain woods, are just there. There are trees that are the quintessence of their landscape—the pointed darker cypresses against the dark blue Italian sky; the flat, protective umbrella of the Kenyan thorn trees; the Caribbean palm springing like a fountain from its round bare trunk; the speckled hide of the great cork trees of Portugal.

The deciduous trees are a perfect architecture of winter, a maze in which the eye travels; endless planes and angles and cross-sections and twiggy outbursts, almost black against the winter sun. And there is something infinitely reassuring in the knowledge of the underground tree—the great horny mass of roots, keeping the rough circumference of the tree in air, a factory of preparation below the cold crust of the earth. Even more assertive, our Baltimore tulip magnolia, the instant its petals have been washed and blown away in April, discloses a thousand buds, tight and battened down for the contest. There they sit, presumably bereft of nourishment for the long months ahead, having an entire summer to go through in the foreknowledge of winter. Later, under the sleet and mud-colored skies, they roost there like demonstrators defying an evil regime.

Well, my friend, unlike Solomon's plaintiffs, will have his half. I hope it is stacked in huge logs in his deprived yard, by the rhododendrons curled up in disgust at February. And that it will end up in one of the most ancient of rites, cremated with respect and gratitude. It will burn strongly and for a long time, having stored up a great richness of resistance. And in my friend's mind, as it settles to its ashes, its great leafy ghost will loft itself into the juridicial Cambridge air.

A Day of One's Own

Artists' colonies, those mysterious sanctums of isolation and peace, seem often to be regarded by the general public as a cross between a manifestation of almost religious obsession and a dubious escape from reality. "Is it really necessary?" friends ask, with polite skepticism, "to go all that way to write?" To sculpt, to paint. They seem to feel this especially in the case of the writer, whose basic equipment is a few notebooks and sheaf of pencils or, at most, a portable typewriter. It seems to them a bit bizarre that no space, physical or mental, can be found for work outside of the difficult-to-achieve boundaries of an elaborately organized system, set up precisely for the artist's needs.

For many writers it is definitely necessary; or, if not necessary in the strictest sense of the word, then a providential aid. In spite of the rare, detached, and untroubled soul capable of an intimidating power of concentration and a husky self-confidence that makes self-assertion second nature, who is able to write in the midst of, or over the prostrate form of, everyone and everything, or of those people who produce six hundred–page novels on commuter trains or on the kitchen table at midnight, the value rings true. It is highly doubtful that a full-fledged genius is going to be thwarted in creativity by any practical circumstances whatsoever, including the comfort or wishes of anyone in the vicinity. But a great deal of fine work—the majority, obviously, of fine work—is done by people who are not geniuses.

Of two classes of artists who need, and use whenever they get the chance, the protection of a colony's environment, the first class (those whose life circumstances make privacy and leisure

---

From *Baltimore Sun,* 16 February 1978.

next to impossible to attain) is obviously the most directly in need. Sometimes a writer in the second (one who is able in her own environment to procure small gobbets of time) feels almost guilty in taking up a place where both of these precious commodities are available to writers starved for them.

But the colonies, wisely, have made it clear that the very purpose of their existence is to provide something even more precious than hard-to-come-by leisure and privacy—and that is the pervading sense of the expectation of serious work. Repeatedly, writers have lamented that in America they often feel themselves so out of the current of daily life as to have the sensation of having developed some basic eccentricity that sets them, in no complimentary sense, apart.

I think mournfully of a conversation I had some years ago with an Elderly Relative. The ER was commenting, with some rancor, that she seldom saw a novelist cousin any more. "Nobody sees her," said the ER. "I just don't know what's the matter with that girl!"

Placatingly, I suggested, "Perhaps she's just so busy working, that. . ."

"Working!" she interrupted, in contempt and revulsion. "That girl's never had to do a day's work in her life. She's just sitting up there writing, writing, writing."

One may opt for laughing lightheartedly, but it is extraordinary how insidiously destructive the milder versions of this innocence can be. Checking into an office at 9 A.M. hurts no feelings; refusal by the writer of an invitation because of "work" often causes a sort of subcutaneous irritation that, if repeated, is cumulative.

The great, the splendid, gift of the colony for the arts is that what outside is a sort of egocentric quirk is, within, the norm. Friendly, aloof, somber, cheerful, grumpy, charming; toehold young, established reputations; all share one thing: a common purpose and a respect for it in others and in themselves. Every writer is terrified of each day's beginning. Lacking the office time clock, the classroom commitment, the writer must overcome, somehow, that vast and passionate urge to do something else—*any*thing else—rather than pick up again the now-chilled, immobile, and resistant mass abandoned the day before, and somehow electrify it back to life, warmth, and its own voluntary motion. It is amazing how this hateful obstacle is softened and shrunk by the common movement. The last cup of breakfast coffee swallowed, the tide is moving in one direction: toward that canvas, that piano, that desk. It is what all are here to do. And the number of those who fake it is infinitesimal. They are here to work, and in their different fashions, their separate tempos, they work.

In the two oldest of the colonies that life goes steadily on, summer, winter; in high rooms looking over elaborate lawns, lily ponds, giant evergreens; or in small studies in the woods, where the replenished fire makes the only sound except for the artist's tools, and the lunch basket arrives furtively outside the door and waits there. No one checks on progress. No one ever, ever, "drops in." The only rule is, no no no visiting, except by specific invitation, for that exact minute.

The troops fall in for dinner weary, laconic, petulant, voluble, exalted. A friend may say, with real interest, "A good day?" (a reversal of the ghastly imperative of the gas station and supermarket, delivered to the rebellious recipient on the rainy dusk of a disastrous eight hours: *Have a good day!*)

Visitors from our discrete worlds, we look at one another: a short story writer (a cook from a French restaurant); a novelist (a British university professor); an essayist (a Sicilian, here with his painter-wife); a poet (chancellor at a state college); a sculptor (a taxi driver); a composer (a tenured member of a music department). For some of us the day has been good only in the degree of freedom to use it. For some it glows with a nimbus. But for each it has been his or her own. And there will be another, tomorrow; except for the nervous, reentry-conscious last-nighter, whose gear is packed, for whom someone has bought a valedictory bottle of wine; of whom no one asks, "A good day?"

IV

An Interview and Four Poems

The Sisters

Everyone notices they are inseparable.
Though this isn't quite so, it might well be.
Talk about depending on each other . . .
One can't say they are totally
congenial—irritation isn't unknown.

Yet it is, truly, touching, how they go on
year after year, not just pairing lives but
taking even holidays and vacations together,
sharing what happens to come along.
Here they are in the Caribbean.

Choose a day—the eighteenth of March for example:
they awake at almost but not quite
the same instant, disoriented:
where is the east? where anything else?
But they aren't going to dog each other all day.

B, anyone would have to admit,
is the better adjusted—easily pleased.
What marvelous lobster! she cries.
Smell the air! (The island is full of spices
and the air is soft as well as fragrant.)

A's energy always seems to be erratic:
first she's on and on about something,
then she wants a nap. She's a great sleeper
and has been known to cast away
hour after precious hour asleep without shame.

And she gets fixations—dashing off
to some spot they've already seen,
and talking about it when she gets back.
Take the little group of graves by the Old Men's Home
the station-wagon passes on its way to the beach.

Both of them noticed it—how could they help?
It's a little patch, unfenced, with four or five
graves. One apparently new and covered
with brightness. They even both waved
to the four old men on the porch who waved back.

But later, it turns out, *A* went back by herself,
sharp-eyed as ever, to examine the yellow
and violet cellophane, the rubber pond-lilies
floating on dust; the whole glittering heap
of rainbow mound; even asked questions.

That happened this morning; with the result
that when *B* swam in the sea—that sea
like a sapphire flawed with gold and green—
A went to sleep. The time she wastes
like that, slack as a weed in a wave!

This means that tonight she'll keep *B* awake
probably for hours, prowling about.
But they fight less than most sisters
and when the question of separation once arose
you should have seen them recoil—both, both.

At Scrabble this afternoon they played partners:
tiles smooth to the fingertips, words appearing,
solid as objects—*salmon, cat;* or abstract,
as *who, why, go.* They did very well.
Then *A* wouldn't participate in the talk at dinner.

On the whole, this was a good day; hard rain
rattled the roof, then the real rainbow threw up its arch,
and amicably they watched the blood-orange dip
into water; then stars, larger and brighter than elsewhere.
Before bed, *A* looked at herself in the mirror, using *B*'s
eyes.

A Conversation with Her Sister

An Interview with John Wheatcroft

Wheatcroft: How old were you when you started writing poetry?

Jacobsen: I would think, probably, around eight or nine years old, because a magazine that you are much too young to have ever heard of, *St. Nicholas Magazine,* which was a very distinguished national child's magazine, published my first poem when I was eleven.

And did you keep writing consistently then, or was there a hiatus between that precocious writing of poetry and the time when you started as an adult poet?

No, there really wasn't any hiatus. I wrote some perfectly awful poetry regularly for years, a long time. I started publishing in the *Junior League* magazine when I was eighteen or nineteen. Then, really, I suppose when I was in my early twenties, I began writing what I would consider any part at all of my serious work.

Even though a person's a born poet, there have to be some models, and I wonder, at eight and nine, what were your models for poetry?

Well, I had a very, very curious childhood, educationally speaking. I didn't go to school until I was fourteen, and what I did was read immensely. My mother, I think very wisely, placed no

---

From *Our Other Voices: Nine Poets Speaking* (interviews), ed. John Wheatcroft (Lewisburg, PA: Bucknell University Press, 1991).

restrictions on what I read, she let me read what I could enjoy and what was around the house. I went from Rudyard Kipling and Robert Service through Blake and the very early poets, a little Milton, which I abandoned very rapidly at that age. Right now I could sit here and recite—I promise I won't—but I could sit here and recite Robert Service by the hour. It's amazing; I think those things that you memorize, particularly something like Service, with that unforgiving rhythm, you do remember. I read just the most widely heterogeneous kind of material, anything that I could put my hands on. I read Shelley and Keats very early. I read a lot of awful poetry that was in current anthologies; I mean it didn't seem that awful, but now, I think, as our tastes have changed, that it would seem pretty bad. So there was no pattern to it at all.

And who were the poets of the twentieth century that you first ran into?

It's all such a jumbled mass in my mind, the poetry, that it's really a little hard to remember. Very few, until I went to school, very, very few. My mother was a great reader, and she was a highly intelligent person. She was also completely uneducated in the sense that we think of education. She went to a girls' finishing school. She never went to college. She didn't care particularly for poetry. It wasn't something that she read for pleasure. But she was a tremendous reader. She read biography; she read philosophy as much as she was able; she read novels. Yet she read very little poetry. She was, however, very fond of William Butler Yeats, so, naturally, that was an early influence that never went away. Yeats was one of the big poets in my life.

Yeats and Auden I know you've mentioned elsewhere as influences on you.

Yes. I didn't come to Auden until shortly before I met him. I was the president of the Maryland Poetry Society, which was then something that I think of as very pious and is no longer organized the same way. Instead of having poetry read by members, we have some fine poet come to read three times a year. Well,

Auden did come down to Baltimore. That was when I was in my late twenties. By that time I had found people who meant a great deal to me. Keats, for example, has meant an enormous amount. I didn't really run into . . . did you say nineteenth or twentieth?

Twentieth century.

I didn't really run into any sophisticated twentieth-century poetry until I was almost in my twenties. In other words, I had begun writing and even publishing here and there before I had anything except an anthology acquaintance with twentieth-century poets.

Well, let's back up into the nineteenth century. How about Emily Dickinson? When did you run into her poetry?

Fairly late, again. I'm trying to think of the people with whom, by the time I was twenty years old, I felt I had any kind of an affinity with at all. As I've said, I think immediately of Yeats; he was the great person. When I discovered Auden, it was like discovering a whole new world. He made an enormous impression on me. I think that the first thing that struck me was the incredible variety that he used, the range of what he had done. That simply bowled me over. I didn't have any twentieth-century women poets as models in those early days. I didn't discover Louise Bogan and Elizabeth Bishop for years.

You know, the years of reading poetry tend to meld together. It's very hard to pinpoint the age at which this or that happened. When I went to school, which I did at the age of fourteen, we studied almost entirely nineteenth-century poets. I didn't have in my English class, for instance, really any twentieth-century exposure whatsoever. A little Elinor Wylie, a little Edna St. Vincent Millay, but it was almost entirely Shelley and Keats and that whole vintage.

Do you think that, formally, when you did run into, let's say Dickinson, who was doing things very differently from the Victorian poets, that she did have any influence on your use of rhyme, for example?

You know, when people ask me about influences, it is so hard. I think so many influences are subliminal. Things show up in the most extraordinary way in your work, when you're really not conscious of reading something and saying, yes, I'd love to try to do something like that. I can't think of modeling myself on someone. I've read poems and said, that would be fun to try to do, but the people that I came to admire most I wasn't exposed to at an early age. Elizabeth Bishop is, to me, just a superb poet. I went through a phase of being devoted to both Elinor Wylie and Edna St. Vincent Millay. After a while I got bored with both of them. Then I came back. In recent years I've come back to feel that Millay was dropped more completely than she should have been. I think people remembered stuff like "My candle burns at both ends" and lost track of some of the sonnets and some of the core of really gutty work that she did. But at that point I had some fairly inferior models, I think. As for those poets who were important to me, I suppose I would have to say Yeats, Auden, Roethke; I'm trying to remember when I began to read Roethke, because he was one of my—he still is one of my favorites.

You have a poem called "The Edge." Does that owe anything to Roethke's "The edge is what I have"?

There, again, I can't answer that, not consciously, not consciously in any way. But I know that my poetry changed after each impact with a splendid strange new poet, not in ways so that I could say to myself, ah, now you see, that's because I've been reading so and so, but that it did change. I think that such impact stretches your concept of what can be done. Above all, it educates your ear in ways that you aren't always analyzing at the moment. I didn't run into, for instance, Archie Ammons, who is a poet whose work I admire tremendously, until I was in my middle or late thirties. There, again, that is one of the kinds of poetry that had impact. Certainly, his work has made a tremendous difference to me. It's provided me with whole new concepts, great pleasure; I read him and reread him; I admire him enormously; and yet I can't see any practical evidences of influence in my own work.

I'm sure it works at a very deep level.

It does. I really think it does.

In "Genile Reader" you say a poet is "dangerous and steep."

I was reading "Sailing to Byzantium" before I wrote that poem. I laid "Byzantium" down and wrote the poem that night. Of course, it could have been about any other poet, but it happened to be Yeats that I was reading, for maybe the one hundredth time.

Of course, most people wouldn't think of poetry as dangerous at all.

Oh my, you remember Wallace Stevens saying that wonderful thing: "It lies in the sun. Its head is on its paws. It could kill a man." I think it's tremendously dangerous. I think it's a minefield. You walk over it, and suddenly you are precipitated into confronting things that you have never realized existed, have never had in your consciousness. I think poetry is steep; I would say reading it is just like climbing a mountain. You might go off the edge at any minute; it's dangerous. I stick by those two words.

You have, I know, had a life besides the life of a poet. You've had a very gratifying marriage and domestic life, and I'm wondering, in your title poem of your new volume, "The Sisters," is sister A *in any way related to you as a poet? You mention* A'*s energy, for example, and* A'*s an insomniac, isn't she?*

Yes, yes, she's always going over . . .

And you use the word insomniac *in the title of the volume for another poem, don't you? Are you an insomniac?*

I'm what Mr. George Bush would call a card-carrying insomniac. I really am. I've gotten over it a little bit in recent years, but for many years it was a real problem.

Would you write at night?

Quite often. Quite often I would get up and write at night, not as a pattern, and, of course, when it comes to something like fiction, it would be impossible for me, because you can be very disruptive by rushing around the house. You have people getting up and thinking that you're sick, that there's something the matter with you. I have gotten up and written poems at night.

As far as "The Sisters" goes, that's really one of the few poems I think that I've ever written about myself, and, when I say about myself, I mean simply as a prototype of a human being. I've always been fascinated by how very different the selves within yourself are, how you can carry on in one way, making conversation and going out for drinks and doing the marketing, and all the time this other person is having this active, secret subterranean life going on. So I thought it would be fascinating to write a poem about it. I find that the poem is usually read on the level of two separate individuals. There have been some very interesting differences about it. A few people have said right away, well, this is really a poem about what happens to the two selves, but many other people have found it a poem about two human beings making a combination and a life together. I remember one perceptive reader saying when she read "The Sisters": "Oh, I love that poem. You don't know how good it is." She added, "You know, I've got a sister . . . ." And I thought, well, if it works . . .

Robert Frost once said to me—I'd asked him about something that I couldn't see in a poem (not one of his but in another poem), and I said people keep saying this and I really can't see this in the poem—Frost said, well, I always say that a man is entitled to any oil that's found in his backyard. That's how I feel. If it works on that level, fine, I'm happy.

On the other level I'm interested particularly in A. *Emily Dickinson has that wonderful phrase "the self behind the self." That, I think, says it pretty well.*

It does, exactly.

I'm interested in A, who's the self behind the other sister, and she's not only an insomniac; she has great energy; she has fixations. Do you think that for you as a poet you have fixations, obsessions? Do you have a kind of tunnel vision?

Oh, yes. Don't you think most people do have obsessions? Fortunately, they're usually not permanent, enduring ones, but I'm not sure that almost any poem that you're writing isn't obsessive in a way. I think that when you're caught up by this thing and you're struggling with it, or it's beginning just to bud and break forth, everything begins to relate to it. You're seeking it and seeing it everywhere. So I think it has an obsessive quality. I believe the creative process tends to be a little bit obsessive.

Your poems are largely concerned with people. Yet in your poems you move all over the world—Africa, Greece, Grenada, the Mississippi . . .

It sounds so pompous. I hate people whose poems sound like travelogues, but I can't help it.

Venice, Troy, New York. So place is important to you, too, isn't it?

Yes, very.

Africa, the Orinoco. And when you are traveling, are you writing then, are you taking notes, or are you just storing material away in your head and your imagination, your memory?

Really, I think storing away in my memory. I'd find if I went back, I'm pretty sure, that in the bulk of poems—and there are a lot of them that are laid in different cultures and different countries, very few were written on the spot—I think, not to go Proustian, that there's something that accumulates and enriches. It's almost as if you have a seed that's beginning to develop, and it has to be put into the soil, and it has to mature.

Almost all of my poems have been, I wouldn't say "emotion recollected in tranquillity," because I haven't had that much tranquillity in which to recollect, but they have been almost all subsequent to the actual stay in a place. Now, that hasn't always been true. For instance, in Grenada, where I've lived for weeks and weeks on end for years, I've done a lot of writing. But most of the time when I travel, I don't get to a place and say, oh I just know I can write a poem about this place; that doesn't happen. And the poem is not necessarily so much about the place as about the effect the place has on the human being. It's not particularly descriptive; there are descriptive elements in it, naturally, but I have never been able to write nature poetry in the sense of just going to a place and saying, oh how beautiful, let me try to describe it. That I've done very seldom.

You have a poem called "Distance," and in that poem distance is a rather futile, self-protective device. Do you see distance as involved in your process of writing at all? Maybe it's a different concept of distance I'm thinking about. I think of your wonderful poem about the shade seller. How about the shade? Are distance and shade necessary to you—that is, do you need a kind of disengagement from raw experience and getting out of the heat of the sun, and removing yourself a bit away from life raw, so that there is time for reflection? I think of Marvell's "green thought in a green shade." Does that attitude appeal to you at all?

Yes, it does, and, you know, you've said something that has made me think of a brand new aspect of the process. It's rather like "The Sisters"—there are two sides of it; and the distance can mean two almost opposite things. I think there is a visionary kind of distance, the kind of distance that is terribly important, that William Meredith said something about in a wonderful poem that's dedicated to Muriel Rukeyser—I wish I could remember the lines—to the effect that you must always care about people, you must always have the capacity to love, but you must always be able, if you are a writer, to put a small amount of total distance between the poet and the person or object written about, and I think that's true. So that, in that sense, distance is terribly important, for the same reason that I can't suddenly go to a country and begin writing about it; I do have to have distance.

In the other distance that I was thinking of—it's really fascinating—I suppose it's the closeness that's scary. In other words, that human beings have this distance between them that is important. Then, on the other hand you have actual physical distance in which the most horrendous things can be happening. I think everybody now is having this very coarsening and terrifying experience, sitting around with a martini or in front of the fire and turning on the television, because you want to know what's gone on during the day, and seeing and hearing appalling things, I mean really appalling things happening all over the world; degrees of suffering and humiliation and torture that your mind can't even take in. And you finish your martini and go into dinner. That must have some sort of profound effect on us.

I often wonder what's happening to us; it does give us that kind of obliviousness, it seems to me, that insects have or that certain kinds of animals have. As long as something isn't happening right in front of your eyes and you can't reach out and touch it, you have an ability to shut it off, to pull down a shade, and I suppose that's absolutely necessary. I mean, if five of the disasters that you read about happened on your front porch or in your living room, you'd be a wreck for years.

So distance, well, it's like the two sisters: there's the beneficent distance that is necessary, that is precious between people and between the concept and the execution, and then there's the distance that seals you off from the emotional experiences of other people, and that I think is becoming more and more dangerous to us. I'm wondering how good it is for you to pick up your paper every day, read these things, have them in front of your eyes, and just shrug them off, which you have to do in order to go on living. I don't think other generations have ever had a similar predicament. Such horrors were filtered through physical distance; there was certainly no visual, absolutely no visual contact. It's a brand new danger.

About a year and a half ago I was flying from Crete to the mainland of Greece, in a little plane, and, as we flew over the Sea of Crete, I saw far below us a ship, and for a moment it occurred to me that it would be easy to drop a bomb on that ship, and that it would seem like nothing more than target practice. I wonder whether those who have to drop the bombs and push the buttons, if they had to be right there and see the flesh coming apart and the blood spurting out, they'd be able to do it.

Exactly, exactly. Do you remember Count Ciano's famous remark about how he bombed something and it exploded, and he said it looked like a giant rose, it was so beautiful. Exactly, exactly.

To follow along that line a bit, do you think that poetry does have some effect on our moral sensibilities, individually, and does it in any oblique way affect us collectively as moral beings? That's a tough question, I know.

Well, it is. Auden, of course, said that poetry makes nothing happen. I don't believe that. I don't think that's true. I think it does make things happen. Something that is absorbing me very much at the moment, and I wish I could turn it into poetry in some way, is the connection between art in its purest form, its most beautiful form, which has to be, it seems to me, an ennobling and enlarging experience, and the fact that the sense of art has so often dwelt so strongly in people of great cruelty and really very, very bad qualities. The tomb that has been uncovered recently has fascinated me—I don't know if you've been reading about it—but I believe it's the oldest, next to King Tut's, that's been discovered, and this warrior-priest was buried with an ornament that is so exquisite that they described it at great length. I won't try to go into it—but apparently it is flawless in its beauty. But what it actually depicts is a bound prisoner of war with his hands lashed and his head bowed, and the king warrior has him by the hair and is getting ready to cut his throat. And the thing is so beautiful.

To me that is a perfect paradigm of what baffles me: that something can be exquisite, obviously executed exquisitely and appreciated by the king as an exquisite thing of beauty, which in itself, it seems to me, should be releasing and ennobling, and yet there's no connection; it's cut completely off from what we would think of as the ethical or moral sense. Of course, it's hard to put ourselves back in the kind of culture in which this didn't seem to be a moral problem. It was probably an ecclesiastical habit; this was what the priests did in order to make the sun rise or the rains come or something, but I've noticed that in actuality, very often, someone who would spend half an hour arranging a wisteria spray in a beautiful vase, praising beauty, praising delicate fragile beauty, would go out and order a torture session. It's a very mysterious and fascinating thing to me. I think art has to be ennobling. I can't believe it isn't, but the effect is certainly not a direct one, two, three process. I don't know. What do you think about it? Is the interviewee allowed to question the interviewer?

Of course.

It's a real problem.

I had a rather fanciful idea after World War II, which was rather violent for me, and while we were in the Cold War and very fearful that a third world war might break out. At that time I was seriously listening to the late Beethoven quartets for the first time, and I had the fond idea that if we could just get the leaders of the world to sit down and listen together, before they'd begin to negotiate, to that wonderful B-flat quartet, then they would negotiate. It's a fanciful idea, I know, yet I wish that it would work that way.

You're talking about exactly what I'm driving at.

I'm not sure that those leaders weren't all, in our sense, tone-deaf.

Yes, I think that's true, but then you go back to some of the musicians who created those things, and you would expect them to be moral supermen, yet, as we know, this is not always the case. It's a very mysterious thing to me, and it really hit me this time, and I've been wondering about it and thinking about it and wishing I could put it into proper words, this side-by-side simultaneous existence of the most exquisite humility toward beauty and the most profound callousness toward what we would regard as moral and ethical issues. It's a fascinating anomaly.

It's a variation on your sisters theme . . .

Exactly, exactly.

Except the two selves are radically different in a moral way, rather than in their habits.

Maybe I can write "Sisters II" like "Rambo." (*Laughs.*)

A little question, just because it piqued me: I noticed that the epigraph to "Trial Run" comes from Langland's Piers Plowman. *What took you to* Piers Plowman?*—a poem that I much admire.*

I hadn't read it. I keep coming back to the fact of the weirdness of my education. I hadn't read that until I was about, I guess I must have been in my late forties, and I was fascinated by it. To begin with, it represented a kind of poetry that I wasn't familiar with, and then I just found it very powerful and very direct, and it meant a lot to me. Evidently, then, I never read it again; I forgot all about it. But it's interesting—we were just talking about whether things are subliminal or not. Well, Langland's poetry stuck with me, and the whole thing fascinated me. All those myths are very productive for the poet, I think. This idea of the workmen who labored over the ark and then saw it go tooling off without them—that's symbolic to me, also, of so many things that happen in life. There's the person, the creator, that launches this thing, and it goes on and speaks to people or does what it's supposed to do, and they are left in the flood.

Of course, Langland never even affixed his name to his poem, and for many years no one was absolutely certain that Langland was the poet.

I didn't know that. How did they finally authenticate it?

It was authenticated in the twentieth century by modern scholarship. I'm not sure exactly how.

I didn't know that.

Of course, we still don't know who was the wonderful poet who wrote Sir Gawain and the Green Knight *and* Pearl, Patience, and Purity, *either, just as we don't know the architects for those great cathedrals.*

Do you think that we ever will know the writers of those poems?

I don't think so. I fear that's beyond recovery.

After such a long time, how do things like that come to light—some paper that hasn't been discovered or some manuscript that slipped through somewhere?

Often it's accident or serendipity. Sometimes a scholar will sit down to try to make a discovery, but rarely will it happen in that way.

I know that at one time you were much interested in drama and did some acting, as a matter of fact. What influence has your interest in drama and the stage had on your writing of poetry?

Well, I think it's probably had more influence on my fiction, but it's also considerably affected my poetry. The theater was my great love. When I was seventeen I had life completely worked out, no problems whatsoever; I was going on the stage. I'd be a professional actress. But then, after all, you don't act all day, everyday; I was going to write poetry on the side. So, you know, I had about as much conception of what physical energy and despair and everything else being an actress involves as if I were an unborn child.

But I did act in the civic theater in Baltimore. There was a theater called the Vagabonds, which was the original little theater, the oldest little theater. It's still going, but it's, I won't say it's fallen on evil days, but it's far from what it was then. Then it was really almost the only alternative we had to musical comedies. The two main theaters in Baltimore brought in New York musical comedies. The Vagabonds was the only organization doing serious theater, and it was a marvelous organization. It was, you know, known all over the country. I remember going to California when I was in my early twenties, and when I met anyone out there who cared anything about the theater, the first thing they would say was, you're from Baltimore, tell me, do you know the Vagabonds?

My brother, who was a very talented actor, and indeed was on the professional stage for some years, got me a little part. I think

I brought in the tea tray or something, when I was still at school, and I was able to do this because they were—I don't know what you would call them—they were not professionals, and they were certainly not amateurs. They were a group, most of whom had worked together for years. They were all people who worked in other fields, so they had to rehearse at night, which they did for three weeks before every play, and then they played six nights a week for three weeks, so that six weeks were involved in every play.

From the age of about fifteen until I got married at twenty-three, I worked regularly with them. In the classic way I toiled my way up from being a maid in a white apron. I finally did a couple of juvenile leads, to my great joy. In fact, I think probably one of the thrills of my life happened during the Vagabonds' twentieth or twenty-fifth year celebration. They took over the big theater in Baltimore, which was then Ford's Theatre, and they were putting on *The Truth about Blades.* There's only one feminine part in *The Truth about Blades,* so I was not a star by brilliance, I was a star by accident. At any rate I went into that huge theater, where we played for one week, and had the star's dressing room. To this day I don't remember anything more thrilling. But it was a very brief career. The reason I stopped that—I got married. My husband, obviously, was working during the daytime, and we simply would not have seen each other for six weeks. A Vagabond production was a very seriously done thing. The Vagabonds was a wonderful organization. I loved the theater.

Although I haven't done it as much in the past year, because it's been a very strange, hectic year, I usually go to New York at least twice a year and just have an orgy of theater. We have one of the best theaters in the country now in Baltimore's Center Stage, which, along with the Arena Theatre in Washington and a couple of others, is really outstanding. They are highly professional, not stocked with local players. I think my feeling for the theater has probably had a big effect on the fact that my poems to some degree are almost always little stories; not in that they have, necessarily, characters and plot, but that they have motion, that they start at one place and end in another, I hope, and there is, I try to feel, nothing static about them. I think that's because the theater has had a great influence on me. In the theater something works up to some kind of a climax; you learn something; you know something when you go out of the theater that you didn't know when you came in, ideally. I think that's had a big effect on my work, both fiction and poetry.

You mention energy in poetry. Your poetry does have a great deal of energy, and I suspect one of the reasons for it is that, even though it is not narrative or dramatic poetry, there's a sense of narrative or drama in the poetry. It seems to me that whether you're writing drama or narrative or poetry, if you can recapture something of that very early time when there was no distinction among those three genres, then you energize the piece even more. Your poetry does that. I always sense something dramatic in the poem. In your stories you have just a splendid ear for dialogue. It's very precise. Have you tried writing drama at all?

I never have, but I'd love to. Obviously, there's not going to be time to launch myself in a completely new genre at this point, but I've always thought that to write a good play and actually see it acted before your eyes would be one of the great thrills of writing. I have never tried to write a play. I think I'm so swamped by trying to swing a normal human life, and be a poet, and be a short story writer, that I'm simply terrified of trying to learn a new form. I'm not a person who believes that just through some kind of talent that can be nurtured you can suddenly plunge in. I know enough about poetry, and I know enough about fiction, to understand that you've got to know what you're doing. You've got to learn the rules; not that you will live by them, but you have to have that basic knowledge. I know so little, structurally, about theater; my only connection with it is simply as theatergoer. I've never never tried to do the thing itself. I don't promise that I never will. I would love to, but I have seen so many terrible plays.

I have a number of friends who have dabbled in this kind of thing and even have had plays produced in small theaters, and I have seen that there is such a difference between being a good writer of prose or even a good poet and being able to pull together a play in which everything is concentrated right there before your eyes, where you can't stop and tell the audience anything, where it's got to be acted out, and there has got to be that constant tension. I'd love to try it. Maybe someday I will, but, then, when you think that you make a little way in your own fields, the idea of storming another barricade is so overwhelming. I think I'm much too fatigued to try it.

I know you have spent considerable time at Yaddo and the MacDowell Colony. I suppose that writers' colonies are your way of getting distance and getting into the shade so that you can do some writing. But, except for poetry readings, you've stayed out of the academy. Is there a particular reason for that? Do you think that academy has had a deleterious effect on poetry?

Well, there are various reasons. I think that came about naturally, to begin with, because of my curious, very curious education. It's not only that I never went to college. Until I was married I never had sense enough to realize that I might want to go. My father died when I was very young, and my mother, who was an extraordinary woman, a very beautiful woman, and a very intelligent woman, and talented in many ways, was the most strange amalgam of the ideas of the old South and her own intellectual forays. She thought that college was a necessity for a boy. It would never have occurred to her that her son wouldn't go to college, and indeed he did. It never occurred to her that her daughter would.

I often have thought of Tennessee Williams. I think mother felt—she would probably not have put this into words—that for girls who have absolutely no Gentleman Callers, and obviously were never going to have any Gentlemen Callers, it would probably be a very good idea to go to college. It would fill in that gap that had been so lamentably left by life. But I was having a very good time. I matured in the most weird, lopsided way. I mean, I think I matured mentally quite early, but I matured slowly in other ways, so that, when I was seventeen or eighteen, it never occurred to me that it could be important that I go to college, that I would get all kinds of things at college that I would not get by going to New York and trying to go on the stage and write poetry. And mother used to be called out periodically by the headmistress of my school, who would say, "Mrs. Boylan, you know, really, this child is college material, and you really ought to reconsider this decision." Then my mother would say to me, "You don't want to go to college do you?" And I'd say, "No, I don't want to go to college." (*Laughs.*)

It was really perfectly fantastic. So to say that I didn't have an early rapprochement with the academic world is putting it mildly. Then I started dropping poems into mailboxes. The first mature poem I ever had published, except one that was published in *Commonweal,* was published, of all things, by Harriet Monroe. I'd dropped it in a mailbox on the corner. And when Harriet Monroe took it I didn't believe it; I still don't believe it. I can remember to this day the blue single sheet of acceptance that *Poetry* used at that point; I can remember opening the envelope and seeing that.

So that I was more or less launched on the periphery of professional poetry life before it ever occurred to me what I was missing in the academic world. I had no academic contacts of any sort. I knew no poets. I had a very social life, I mean a very lively intercourse with people, so that the academic world, with which I now have a very warm and affectionate relationship—and I've now traveled to innumerable colleges and have a large number of friends who are in that world—all during the early formative period was remote, completely remote to me. It was not a conscious choice; I didn't have the input, as we would now say, of "my dear, look, this is what you're going to miss if you don't go to college, if you don't launch in that whole series of contacts, and this is what may benefit you if you don't."

I've never been able to say which choice I should have made, given my own temperament, my own life, and the unique quality of my poetry. When I say that, I don't mean the poetry is unique; I mean how strange my approach has been. Recently I've noticed that in the reviews of my late poems, the poems of the last ten years, how often the reviewer has said, "One thing that has served her well is that she has been tenacious about following her own course, and she has avoided all trends." Well, it's probably less that I've avoided all trends than that I was very late in being exposed to any trends, so that lack of academic involvement was not thought out or chosen; it just happened.

But, of course, you're thoroughly educated; you're widely read; you're cultivated; and you're a good example of the fact that you don't need to go to the university to get an education. What I was really thinking about, too, is what about the effect on those who do go to the university, who want to be poets and find themselves involved in creative writing programs? Do you think that they have had a positive effect on developing young poets in this country?

I've never thought a lot about that, because I have so many friends who have been involved in creative writing. And, of course, when you go to colleges all over the country, very often you come there sponsored by the department of creative writing, so I meet a lot of teachers. In fact, when I was poetry consultant at the Library of Congress, we had a national convention on the value or lack of value of creative writing seminars. It was most interesting. We had people from all over the country. We had the Iowa writing group; we had Wallace Stegner; we had Elliott Coleman. Each head of a creative writing department brought a prize student or a prize teacher to give his or her point of view about the thing. And after three days of talk, nobody had decided anything. In other words, what a great many people felt, and certainly what I felt, was that there was, very definitely, a downside to this whole tremendous explosion of creative writing classes all over the country. And I think the downside would be that you have to have a rather strong individual gift, a rather strong sense of your own possible worth, not to be invaded, to a certain degree, when you are part of a peer group who are working with a teacher who will have his or her own concept of writing. And then there's the competition, not to please that teacher, because a good teacher doesn't just want to be pleased, but nevertheless there is a certain constriction because of competition, I think. That's one disadvantage—that you may learn certain concepts that you feel have to be followed, that you may be a little timid about doing something that seems so different from what the people who are admired around you are doing. I do think that's a danger.

I think another very tragic danger is that a great many of these young students come out of writing seminars absolutely convinced that they're going to have a writing career, and, as we all know—I don't think the fallout is as bad as it is in the theater—only a very small proportion of them will ever make a genuine national reputation. And I think their experience sometimes engenders a kind of bitterness. They may go into academic life; they may live their whole life through without ever seeing anything they're written in print or maybe in a tiny magazine somewhere. I think there are a lot of illusions fostered, or even delusions fostered, and I think there's a great deal of pressure to conform, not given necessarily by the teacher but just by the fact of that competitive atmosphere. On the other hand, I'm sure that for people who are in isolated places or have not had contact with other writers, a writing workshop can be a very fruitful experience. I know that.

I think the ideal is a place like Yaddo or MacDowell; to me that is such a wonderful thing, because you've got the best of both worlds. You've got a world where everyone around you is geared to the seriousness and the value of what you're doing. In other words, you're doing something that everyone around you says is valuable and is good; you are there to write or to paint or to compose. That it's important and it's natural and it's normal, and you don't feel like a freak. In addition, there is that tremendous stimulus of being around people to whom this is the object of their lives. At the same time there is no pressure. You're not holding peer group sessions. You may read to one another, and you do, and listen to one another and so on, but there isn't the feeling of outside pressure; it's a much more isolated experience. You are much more on your own. There's nothing to tamp down your individual differences, and to me that is why those places are so marvelous. I have nothing but good things to say about them. I realize that not everybody is happy in such a setting. I mean there are people who come and leave right away. They don't like the isolation, the all-day isolation.

It does sometimes seem that our writing programs, especially the graduate programs, produce more teachers of writing who produce more teachers of writing who produce more teachers of writing.

Exactly.

To change direction for just a moment, in a splendid essay of yours on American women poets you say that in colonial America a woman poet was a literate, highly privileged slave. Because the issue is very much at the front of our mind these days, I'm thinking about gender and poetry. Do you think there is sexual difference in poetry? Is there a woman's poetry as distinct from a man's poetry?

There the operative word is *poetry*. I believe that, if you compare a great deal of poetry written by men and a great deal of poetry written by women, certain themes will manifest a definite gender difference. But I don't feel gender in the quality of the poetry or in the tone of the poetry. I think at the present point the issue is exaggerated, because it needed to be. It's like every other breakthrough. There really was a form of slavery—no question about it; women were subjected to a form of slavery. And when something like that breaks down, then I think there's a natural tendency to make the issue itself a subject matter and make that the springboard for everything that's written. That's why, I think, we're getting such a tremendous blast of feminist poetry, a great deal of which, I think, is not very good poetry. But, as far as quality is concerned, I wouldn't make a gender distinction.

As far as the reaction of the reader goes, I wouldn't make the distinction either. I think that the subject matter has tended to be different, but I suspect that's going to narrow very much. In the past the fields in which women operated and men operated were much more separated. Now that difference is daily being lost, and the professions that are open to women, the lives that are open to them, the freedom for good or for ill that is open to them, are going to make available all kinds of themes and subject matter that were not applicable earlier. So I think that gender in subject matter and tone is going to get narrower and narrower.

As far as quality goes, I think that women poets have shown, in just the comparatively short time that they've had the belated amount of freedom that they've had, that gender difference certainly is not a question of quality. I think that the gender gap is being made too much of in poetry now.

I suppose we're faced with the same sort of puzzling relationship we have between poetry and a larger morality when we think of what the responsibility of a woman poet might be, given the history of the treatment and the position of women, what her stance ought to be in this part of the twentieth century. Is it possible to further the cause without being a polemicist or a propagandist?

I was thinking of this very question recently. You come against certain barriers, you change things and change things and change things, and then you still come up against certain barriers; you make enormous medical discoveries, and you prolong life, but death is going to come. And it's the same with gender; there are certain things that you're not going to change, and I believe that, as long as a woman is the only human creature who is going to become pregnant and be able to bring forth a child, many women are going to start a little back in the race for complete flexibility and freedom to devote their lives to anything they choose. Even if you have day care three hundred and sixty-five days a year, even if you have women who decide not to have children, the fact remains that, until men begin to get pregnant and produce children, women are going to have a special gift and problem. There's no way of pretending it isn't so.

In a slightly different direction, again. You've written criticism and essays on poetry. What took you to Beckett, Ionesco, and Genet?

I started with Beckett in the most hackneyed sense, inasmuch as it was *Waiting for Godot* that got me started. *Godot* is what many people who think of Beckett know, simply that and nothing more. I saw the initial New York performance, and it was one of those times when they have a discussion with the audience afterward. I didn't even know the play when I got the ticket. After the performance there was a general discussion, and two or three people got up and talked about the play. I was sitting up in the first or second row of the balcony, and I thought everything that the three people who were talking about it were saying was absolutely wrong. Well, I'm one of those people who has great difficulty in putting up my hand in a crowd and saying now listen to me and I'll get you straightened out. I sat there seething for about twenty-five minutes, thinking I know, I understand this play, and you are all wrong, you are way off in left field, absolutely, yet I never opened my mouth. This experience disconcerted me so greatly that I went back and saw the play again. Then I read it, and I did find that I had this curious affinity.

To begin with, this is perhaps a cliché to say now, but I don't think so many people were saying it at the time, I think Beckett is a poet. When you read his novels or you read anything that he writes, you realize that he is, essentially, a poet, that he has a kind of negative poetry that conjures up things, to my mind, by hinting at the difference between what he is describing and the possibility of what might be. I got very much interested in this dichotomy, so I wrote a critical article. When I showed it to Bill Mueller, a very old friend of mine, who had written a number of books of criticism, he said, "You know, I like that, I haven't read Beckett yet and I think I will." So we both started reading Beckett, the novels and the plays. Then one day Bill said, "I think it would be great if we collaborated on a book about Beckett." I had never collaborated with anybody; in fact, I had never understood how collaboration worked. So I said, "Bill, I don't see how we can do that, because, close friends as we are, we have lots of different ideas, and if we collaborated it seems to me we would have to see exactly eye to eye about everything." Bill said, "Let's have a go at it; you can do the parts that appeal particularly to you, the parts about the actual drama, the parts about poetry, and I would like to take on the underlying philosophy, and the more academic approach." So we wrote the book, and enjoyed it tremendously. We had happy results. It was a small edition, but it sold out, and then it was picked up by Beckett's publishers in England, Faber and Faber. That was fun.

I'd always loved the theater. I had been reading Ionesco, with whom I was quite fascinated at the time, I think probably a little more than I would be now. But again I could take a fresh approach because Ionesco was so different from anything else I had read, and the wordplay was dazzling. I loved it. Genet, too, was obviously a poet, but I thought he was overrated, a very unpopular thing to say, and I'm probably quite wrong, but I did think so. Again, Bill and I seemed to see more or less eye to eye on this, so we decided to do a second book.

Although I enjoyed doing both these books tremendously, the only reason we didn't go on with it is that I found that such writing took a tremendous amount of energy. My life has always been a battle between the available energy and time, time to write poetry and fiction. Poetry, I think, is just pure energy. So I could see very well that I was not going to be able to fit any bulk of criticism into my life, and, when it came to writing either fiction or poetry or writing criticism, there was just no question. I do much less in the way of book reviewing now for precisely that reason. I sometimes do special things, though; I did a long review recently for the *Nation,* and I've done a few articles, but in general I try to stay away both from lectures and from criticism because of the limited time. It's like a budget, you know: you just can't afford the Rolls-Royce.

You're far too modest. You already have produced a considerable body of criticism, I must say.

Yes, but I tend to shirk it.

In the book on Beckett you two explicitly address poetics and epistemology; also in the Ionesco and the Genet books you are concerned with those issues. Do you consciously have a poetics of your own? Do you consider questions of epistemology when you're writing your own poetry or looking back at it?

I'm afraid the more or less shameful answer is that conscious poetic theory has played very little part in my actual composition process. It certainly has played a part in revision and in my trying to get a somewhat objective look at what I've done, but in that field I'm afraid that whatever I am is comparable to someone in baseball whom they call a natural. I don't work consciously with theory or under the restraints of poetic theory when I am writing. For that matter, most of the epistemological parts of the critical books were really handled by Bill, who's very analytical; he's a philosopher, who is very conscious of theory in his work.

Well, deconstruction has been an issue, a burning issue for the past few years. It's even reached the popular press; I think of that article on the Yale deconstructionists in the New York Times Magazine *a year or so ago. Have you paid any attention to the deconstructionists and their theories? They're very much concerned with epistemology and language.*

I have probably the degree of competence and the degree of knowledge of their theories that one gets in reading good articles in the reviews and quarterlies. In other words deconstruction is nothing that I have pursued as a discipline. I have only a very superficial knowledge of it. I think the problem for me is that I know that whatever I am able to write is ingrained in my own reactions, set in my own tone; that no matter how it changes, and it does change, I hope, all the time, it is not in response to theory. Therefore, I read articles on these things as a matter of interest but without any depth of feeling for them at all, and I certainly cannot claim that they have any effect, constructive or otherwise, on my own work.

It seems to me that most of the academic battles that have raged have been valuable in their residue, in what they've left when their stormy period is over, and not in the very often extravagances of the schools in the midst of the contest. The role of theory becomes exaggerated, I think; it extends itself from being an interested theory and an applicable theory to being something that is essential to the poet, and that is what I shy away from.

Do you think that most poets have something of the same attitude toward developments in theory? Most of the poets you know, are they involved in the battle over deconstruction at the present time?

I'm thinking of my own friends who are poets, and, you know, somehow I have a feeling in my bones that this may not be typical, but I do not think they are. Can it be that these are just the poets I happen to know? I'm wary of speaking for them, because when I have been with them we have talked so much of poetry, but very, very little of poetic theory. I'm trying to think—Stanley Kunitz is a poet that I admire enormously. I know Stanley has passionate feelings about everything, political and so on; but

I have no idea how much these theories mean to him. Among the people that I know best, William Meredith, Archie Ammons, Carolyn Kizer, for example, I'm not conscious of burning interest in, or results from, these arguments. Still, I would suspect there are a great many poets, someone like, perhaps, James Merrill or John Ashbery, who might very easily be deeply involved in deconstructive theory. I don't know either well enough to judge truly. What do you think? That's only the second question I've asked you. How about your own poetry?

I think that most poets, as you've put it, wait and absorb. It's not that they're uninformed or unintelligent, but they must do their own work. Only as they can absorb ideas, whether they are philosophical or aesthetic, do the ideas feed into the work. I think any kind of explicit use of critical theory is almost self-defeating, as far as the practice of poetry is concerned.

That's exactly the way I feel. But you know, we're very poll conscious at the moment. So, if you were to take thirty-five good poets, I wouldn't know how it would come out. Although I agree with you, I know I'm peculiarly vulnerable to a nonanalytical approach, because of the kind of beginnings that I've outlined in my own poetry. I'm a very unusual specimen, so I cannot draw much generalization from my own reactions.

I do think that Beckett and Ionesco and Genet all have some connections with deconstructionist theory, the notion that language is unreliable, that meanings are often arbitrary, that we're trapped in language. That's a way of saying, I suppose, that deconstruction isn't quite so new as it claims to be. It seems to me it does have—I think particularly of painting—some beginnings in cubism, the breaking up of the surface. Then, too, Baudelaire talked about the breaking up of the surface of things and rearranging them on the basis of sensibility.

And the switching of the senses, exactly.

But there is, it seems to me, something a little more dangerous in contemporary critical theory as far as literature is concerned. I heard one deconstructionist, when asked whether poetry was dead, reply, "Not poetry, man, literature."

Oh, that's so tiresome. It's just plain tiresome.

Along with such attitudes comes an attack on what has been called the canon. I can't help noting that theological language has been appropriated for poetry.

Yes, isn't that interesting.

The argument is that any kind of canon is necessarily racist, sexist, and political. What do you think about that?

I think there's a lot of nonsense being peddled; I really do. Do you happen to know Nathan Scott's work at all?

Yes.

Nathan is an old friend, and he sent me last week an article on this very point, in which he's saying, I think, virtually, what you are saying. Now he'll probably kill me for paraphrasing him in this way, so don't take it as Nathan's, take it as mine. Anyway, Nathan was saying something to the effect that, as communal values and assumptions break up, there is this inevitable fragmentation in language, as there is in thought, but that there is a process that is inevitable and dangerous, out of which many valuable things can come.

Still and all, you cannot celebrate and enshrine the fragmentation. What you've got to assume is other theories and other values and avoid the famous baby and bathwater. Nathan has very little sympathy with the deconstructionists and the minimalists; he thinks these theorists are being hypertheoretical and that, there again, they're so afraid of not cooperating with their own dominant theory that it can be a very injurious thing. I really think he's right. But, you see, I'm not timid in saying this. It's like someone who in practice functions but who lacks genuine hard-grained academic background, being critical of academicians. So I stand on the outskirts and don't get in with the combatants. But I do agree very strongly with what you've just said. I think too much theory can be a destructive thing, and I think that the oversimplifications are so tiresome. If someone said something like that about poetry and literature, it's nonsense; it's palpable nonsense.

Do you think that we're in a post-absurdist age? I'm thinking again of Ionesco and Genet. Do you think there's going to be an extension of alienation and despair or a reaction against them with a new conservatism and a new orthodoxy and a new limited kind of optimism? Those are terrible questions; I apologize for them.

No, no, they're very interesting.

Can we go beyond Genet's desire for annihilation, for example?

It's impossible to answer, really; therefore, it's an interesting type of question to say something about. I think that the dangerous thing is the swing that you always get. I would like to think that, it's like, really, coming through an illness—you're very weak, and you're very shaken, yet, if you're lucky and you recuperate, you will have learned many things from it. I have a feeling that what we have been through may make us, ultimately, more optimistic, but I think that's a long-range view.

In the short range I see something very scary. I believe that, because we have become so terrified, because we have lost so many both valuable and fake securities, there is a danger of pseudo-optimism, of the kind of thing that we're seeing politically now. People want to feel good, and there may be an optimism, produced by deliberate blindfolding, that can be very scary. I would like to think that we may come through, probably never again to totally united values, certainly not in our lifetime, but to a closer approach to a serious optimism. But I'm very very pessimistic about it, if you can be pessimistic about optimism.

I believe there is a great tendency now for people to behave like children who've been frightened. People want security; they want to bury their heads in someone's lap. I certainly don't intend to get into politics, but I think there's a wide trend, mentally and politically, and in general in the country, to be reassured, to try to feel good, and which in turn spurs people who see through that to hyperpessimism. So it seems we're at a dangerous point of dichotomy, between people who say, hey, aren't you looking? don't you see what's going on? and even tend to exaggerate the danger, if that's possible, because of their consciousness of this tendency to try to feel comfortable, to try to feel that things are on the whole going pretty well.

You've been wonderful putting up with terrible questions. Let me ask you one final, dreadful question, if you don't mind.

You mean the worst is yet to come? (*Laughs.*)

It's the last. As you look around at contemporary poetry, what do you think of its health these days? How do you judge the quality of some of the poets who are a generation or two behind you? What is your response to the work they're doing today? Does it give you cause for optimism so far as poetry is concerned? Obviously, there's great diversity in kind and in quality, but can you make any kind of overall assessment of the direction that you think poetry is going? Do you have any notion of where the mainstream might be?

As for my feeling about the health of poetry at this stage, I seem to be—you've talked about obsession—I seem to be obsessed with the idea of dichotomy, because I think there's a strange process going on. I don't think there's a question that more poetry than ever before is being poured out. Maybe it has something to do with what we talked about earlier, the creative writing classes, but there's an ocean of poetry engulfing the country. A great deal of it is very, very bad. That is obviously inevitable when you have that many self-styled poets writing. It's hard to dredge up from that absolute torrent the good work. Yet I am optimistic about poetry. Although I think that we've never been so deluged with second- and third-rate poetry, trendy poetry, politically proselytizing poetry, point-making poetry, a dismal, dismal tide, I still am convinced that there are great signs of health in current poetry.

I believe you can look over the world now and see, in America—I can't, obviously, speak for the whole world—look over America now and see more than a handful of fine, distinguished poets, poets following their own particular star, not caught up by the trends and the pushes and the shoves. I think we see less of the mountain peaks than of the valleys. I don't believe we have, with possibly one or two exceptions, anything comparable to the greatest poets we've had in the past. In fact, I wonder if it's possible that we will have that particular kind of poetry again. Yet I do believe more good poetry is being written right now in the United States of America than at any period in my lifetime. I truly believe that. Also ten times more horrible poetry.

That's a note on which to end. You've made it most easy for me to ask you some terrible questions.

They've been wonderful questions.

You've been most gracious, and I thank you very much.

I thank you. I've enjoyed every minute of it.

Voyage

Off sand at the edge of bush the ribs
of a fisherman's intentions spring
toward the sea; the old sea shape

stained by rains, gnawed by beach rats,
a copybook illustration, "Aspiration
Versus Attainment." There by the sound of water

the hoarse talk of water, suck and hiss,
this marine intention
more the sea's creature

than that hotel the fathoms float.
Sand's grainy grip tightens
and foliage takes back its wood.

What of the fisherman?
Did he reach the blue glitter?
Are his fingers bone?

The vines are coming.
The vines are coming.
A tendril has touched the keel.

From *New Yorker*, 24 July 1995.

Program

The glass in her hand flares
like a flower. It is cold and clear
and has a slender long stem.

Over the Martini she sees things
just happened. Her grandmother
saw two dead men, husband

and father, though she saw
elaborate coffins. Here the dead
arrive at six o'clock.

They lie in the street
in artless attitudes.
No pan-in to see

if the eyes are closed or not.
Obviously her Martini is blameless,
and she takes small sips,

with a slight shudder, from the chill
of glass, or scene, or both.
From a new angle still they lie.

She is aware of a deeper dismay.
She feels a cold, horny finger—
habit's—gently touch her heart.

She is positive it is happening,
and stares harder at the shapes, but they are gone.
And someone is talking weather.

From *New Yorker,* 20 November 1995.

Piazza di Spagna

Estragon says to Vladimir
(or vice versa) of happiness
recollected in distress: how
unpleasant that must be.

Ah Estragon, ah Vladimir,
discussing loss, the poet's
mother-lode. On the Spanish steps
chill fingers the bone.

As the sun drops and drops,
stare across at the small,
cold, invisible room
where loss has revelled;

where loss's aficionado
labored to grasp and hold
a green felicity,
Apollo's summer look.

Loss has its *son et lumière*
to show what it has got
and means to keep: a hundred poems,
bright blood, a girl.

From *Atlanta Review* (Fall 1995).